I
SURVIVED

Written By:
James C. Thomas

www.dudleypublishinghouse.net
Submissions@dudleypublishinghouse.net

Dedication

I would like to dedicate this book to the love of my life, my wife Yolanda Thomas. This year marks 35 years of marriage and 38 years in an awesome relationship. Thank you for being the apple of my eye. Most importantly, thank you for being the mother of our three children. Just think of when I first met you in Lithonia. You told me you were not interested becase you already had a boyfriend. Just as God would have it, some time later I saw you and your mother walk in my Fathr's church. I knew then that I had another chance. Now look at us. 38 years later and we're still in love. The proof is in our children LaDonna, James Jr., and Jaron. I thank God for the three of them. With a grateful heart, I dedicate this book to you all as well. You all will always be one of the most important parts of my life. My family has been and continues to be one of my motivations to complete this project.

Acknowledgments

I would like to acknowledge the people that encouraged me to do this project, and those who encouraged me to complete it.

My wife and children have encouraged and supported me the entire way. Thank you. I acknowledge you.

To Prophetess Geneshea Davis and my church family, Chosen Generation Outreach International, who were some of the firsts to approach me about writing this book. Thank you all.

To my siblings and their spouses. To my nieces and nephews. I must admit. I didn't feel confident in my writing abilities. But my neice, Jennifer Harvey, was very instrumental in convincing me that I could do this, and she was right. Thank you.

Thank you to everyone that has supported me during this project. You all have truly been a blessing to me.

Table of Contents

Foreword

It is my humble pleasure to congratulate my father, my Overseer and my role model on his first book. It has been an overwhelming delight to see my father survive it all. This book will be a monumental statue for the world to learn survival techniques. It is a step by step guide on how to win in this life as it will produce difficult times. Full of hope, delight and transparency. I decree and I declare that this is only the beginning of a great thing. Philippians 1:6 says, "Being confident of this very thing, that he which hath begun a good work in you will perform it until the day of Jesus Christ".

Peace & Love

Pastor James C. Thomas Jr.

Introduction

I survived. Yes, I survived. As a human being on this earth, you are always bound to go through a number of challenges. The tribulations may even be more severe for Christians. This is contrary to the belief of most Christians that once you are born again, all your problems have been solved. Well, the scripture tells us that all things work together for good to those that love God. Christians tend to only believe this part of the bible when the going is good, but when it gets tough, the question becomes, "Lord, why me?" Let me tell you something if I am still alive and kicking after everything I have been through, trust me; you can survive just about anything. Everyone faces different types of battles, and some are definitely tougher than others, but no matter what you face, you can overcome them. You need to start seeing any trial and tribulation that comes your way as a moment of testing, as long as you are a true Christian and you believe in God. The trials and tribulations you face today are there to strengthen you for tomorrow's success. Christianity is like travelling on the sea. You cannot expect a smooth sail all through. There will definitely be storms, waves, icebergs, dangerous rocks, and strong winds to make sure the sail is not smooth. In our Christian life, there must be obstacles, challenges, and difficulties along the way. What do we do when trials and tribulations come? How do we prepare ourselves for the challenges ahead? We need to persevere and have faith. This can be likened to the situation the disciples were in when they were crossing the Sea of Galilee. Jesus was asleep even when the storm was raging while the disciples panicked. After Jesus steadied the storm, he rebuked his disciples for their lack of faith. Look at it this way; once you become a believer and have accepted Christ as your Lord and personal saviour, you have been saved from eternal damnation. The Holy Spirit comes into your life to dwell and help you strengthen your relationship with God.

The Holy Spirit is also the comforter that leads believers into all truth. But accepting Jesus Christ as your Lord and personal saviour is the first step to salvation. The next step is building faith. Now how does one build their Christian faith? Through overcoming trials and tribulations.

What is survival?

According to the layman, survival is simply the continuous existence of something in spite of whatever ordeal, accident, or difficult circumstances. Relating it to our Christian life, survival is simply living through all the trials and tribulations that we face in our daily lives. To most people, survival is just overcoming the devil and his antics, but this is not always the case. Whether one is a believer or not, trials and tribulations must come. So if the trials and tribulations come to an unbeliever, would it be termed an attack from the devil? As a Christian, I believe that it is not right to just say that you are under attack from the devil. I say this because admitting that you are under attack from the devil places you under his authority. As born-again believers, we are not under Satan's authority; ever. We are under God's; and if a trial come it is because God ordained it or allowed it. In real-life situations, the stronger one most likely attacks the weaker ones, so when a believer says the devil is attacking them, the believer is giving the devil the upper hand. Take, for instance, Job's case. He didn't know God gave the devil the power to do anything to him without touching his soul. But he kept his faith, and in the end, he came out victorious. It can be assumed that the mere thought of being attacked by the enemy already puts you in a disadvantageous position, and nobody would want that.

God wants all Christians to develop our faith in Him through trials and tribulations, put our spiritual principles to practice, and glorify Him as we overcome these challenges.

We need to understand that it is not the will of God to let these trials and tribulations knock us down. In fact, it is the opposite. Jeremiah 29:11 reads that, "The thoughts of God for us are thoughts of good and not of evil; to give us an expected end." So trials and tribulations are actually meant to raise our spiritual levels. Have trials, challenges, tests, and tribulations kept you from fulfilling what God wants for you? That might be because you need a shift in perspective. You're viewing your trials with the wrong lenses. It is understandable when we get frustrated and tired due to the trials and tribulations, but the word of God is there to give hope to the downcast. The bible says in Isaiah 40: 31 that, "Those who wait on the Lord shall renew their strength; they shall mount up with wings as eagles; they shall run, and not be weary they shall walk, and not faint."

We can draw inspiration from the story of Joseph. Joseph persevered through the trials and temptations that came his way, and he was rewarded in the end. Personally, I like to see the trials and tribulations that come my way as a process of purification. Precious metals like silver and gold go through the process of melting and heating before they become as beautiful as we see them. So when a true Christian goes through hard times, as long as they persevere, they tend to come out better and stronger in the Lord. Job suffered a lot of trials and temptations, but when it was all over, he got everything he ever wished for and more.

Don't misinterpret your season or situation.

Christians need to understand that going through trials and tribulations is not always an attack from the devil. Well, in some cases, it might be actual warfare from Satan, but have you ever sat down to think that maybe you are not doing something right? The truth is, God rebukes (course corrects) His children in various ways, and only a true Christian will understand that some of these hard times may just be ways God is using to draw His children closer to Him. "God chastens (corrects) those that He loves." Now, before you check-out on me, it's important we learn to look at correction differently. It is not God saying we are unworthy or not good enough. It is actually God saying, "I love you enough to spend my time course correcting you." Let us use Jonah as a case study. We all know the story "Jonah and the fish." God called him to Nineveh to do His work, but Jonah refused. We don't really know why Jonah refused, but he did. It could've been because of fear. It could've been because of prejudice or arrogance. No one really knows, but like many of us, Jonah felt he had good enough reason to defy the orders of God. What happened next? He kept facing challenges upon challenges until he finally did what God asked him to do. What if that is the case with that Christian that is facing numerous challenges at the moment? Could it be God talking to him or her and calling them back to Himself?

There was this story I heard about a young man who God was trying to call. He had his own plans for himself, but God had better plans. This young man wanted to be a professional footballer, and he was pretty good at it. However, God wanted him to be something more. During one of the games he was playing, he had an injury that put him out of action for a very long time. After the surgery, he had to stay a while in the hospital to heal. When he thought he was getting better, the doctors dropped a bombshell; he was never going to play the game again. It took him some weeks to recover from the shock, and he had no choice but to turn to God for solace. During that time, he genuinely gave his life to Christ, and guess what, he is now a man of God. We can gather from this story that maybe God was trying to call him to serve Him, but he refused.

Every human being born into this life has a specific purpose he or she has to fulfill. Of course, as humans, we could have other plans, but there is this popular saying that goes, "Man proposes, God disposes." God wanted him to win souls, and there was no escaping it. Some may view it as an extreme measure, but parents will never want to let their children go astray and be willing to use whatever means necessary to save the child. If earthly parents can do anything to save their children, how much more God who loves us so much?

So, as Christians, the sooner we begin to understand that some of our hard times are God's way of telling us that we are on the wrong path, the stronger our faith becomes. Whenever you experience hardships, you should take this first step. Look at your life and find out what you are not doing that perhaps God may be asking of you. As we discussed in the story of Jonah, he knew he was going the wrong and that God was trying to correct him. If you read through that story, you will realize that Jonah knew he was the cause of the troubled storm out at sea. Now, it took him some time, but he finally realized that only God could save him. When he realized that and prayed to God from the belly of the fish, God made the fish spit him up on the shores of Nineveh. This simply highlights what we discussed earlier; God uses His own ways to call His children back to order. It is not good for our Christian faith if we keep believing that every trial and tribulation that comes our way is of the devil. It could be God correcting us. It could even be a test to strengthen our faith. This leads us to the next question to consider.

What is a test?

The English dictionary describes a test as any procedure intended to establish the performance, reliability, or quality of something. Well, the same definition applies to the test of our faith. In Christianity, faith will inevitably be tested.

Saying, "I am a child of God," just doesn't cut it. You need to have more than the words of the mouth type of faith. Declarations without action and actual growth won't profit you much.

A true believer will describe a test as a trial or circumstance that God permits to come your way to help you grow in faith. Like in the general educational system, you cannot go to the next level without a test or examination. So without a test, no matter how strong it is, you cannot move to the next level of your spiritual life. Abraham became the father of all nations because of one attribute; mountain-moving faith. How many of us would have passed the test Abraham was given? Imagine having just one son and being asked to use him as a sacrifice. Most Christians would have attributed it to the voice of the devil, giving him an upper hand in your life. But Abraham had faith in the God he worshipped, and in the end, he did not sacrifice his son, and he won God's heart.

We can say that a test is God's way of knowing how loyal someone is to Him. It may not seem like it, but the tests a true Christian experiences is a way to help them grow in the faith. In those times you are facing your tests, many things may run through your mind, and it is normal. However, you can always go down on your knees and ask God to give you the strength to pass this test. I, for one, have gone through a lot of tests, and I believe I came out better and stronger in the faith, just like a metal that has been refined.

God does not give anyone a load too much to carry. In fact, He said in Matthew 11:28, "Come to me, all ye that labour and are heavy laden, and I will give you rest." That does not sound like a God that will let His people go through tests that they cannot overcome. When the tests come, think of this; God will not give me a load I cannot carry, and this is a test He is using to prepare me for something greater. With that thought comes solace and the strength to carry on and come out of the fire unburnt. Now, it's important that you know this is not always easy. Sometimes you're going to have to practice this train of thought over and over again. And there will be times you don't feel very uplifted as you rehearse this way of thinking. There are going to be time you're going to feel like just crumbing in the floor. And my friend, I want to encourage you in this very fact. It is alright. Cry, wail even if you have to. Give yourself the time to process as a human, but don't stay there for long. You've got to eventually get up and walk in full mountain-moving faith. When you survive your tests and trials, you will see yourself becoming an inspiration and source of hope to those around you. Now, I can confidently tell people something about hope and keeping faith. Why? Because I was able to survive my recent tests by the grace of God.

Survival Of the Fittest

Survival! Survival!! Survival!!!

According to the theories of one of the most outstanding scientists to ever live, survival of the fittest is a natural animal instinct. But what exactly is survival of the fittest? In plain terms, we can say survival of the fittest is just when the stronger thrive at the expense of the weaker. I have said before that I had survived a lot, which means you can also survive. The world is full of trials and tribulations. As Christians, we are bound to face some, and we are *expected* to survive. The question is, how does one survive if they are not strong enough? This is where the idea of "Survival of the fittest" comes into play. We can start with this statement, "Survival is not an opportunity to panic." Some would wonder what I mean by that, and I will explain this in a minute.

When trials and tribulations come into our lives, our basic instinct is to survive. But most Christians start to panic when it is time to fight for survival. Nobody is saying that fear is not natural but take, for instance, someone in the sea who is about to drown. Experts will tell you that struggling in the water may make you drown faster, but the human instinct would definitely make one struggle, especially if the person does not know how to swim. Panic sets in, and panic is a quicker killer than the actual water is. Now, let us relate this idea to our Christian life. We, as Christians, can be seen as that person in the sea, and the sea can be likened to our trials and tribulations. God is the expert, and what does the expert say? Keep calm, or you will drown very fast. In fact, too much struggle will make it a whole lot difficult to help you. So when I say that survival is not a time to panic, what do I mean? I mean that in the sea of tribulations and trials, instead of struggling and drowning fast, you can always look up to God, who is our source of refuge. You need to understand that no matter what we are going through, God is watching us, and He is not going to let His children be overcome by these problems. So why panic? Sometimes, whenever I am down and troubled, all I have to do is remember that God is watching me, and He will never let me down. With this thought comes a feeling of triumph already, and I want you to start doing the same.

What you must understand as a Christian is that any trial that comes your way is not there to kill you or tear you down. First, we must remember that no matter what happens, the Lord is well aware of it. He is the Alpha and Omega, the one who knows the end from the beginning. So we can agree that He already knows of whatever situation anyone is going through. He allows these things to show us who we truly are. There is this saying that goes, "You never know how strong you are until being strong is the only option you have." In those times of trials and tribulations, most people become aware of what God has planned for them. These times also reveal what we're made of, and if we can stand to do some more growing in order to get to the fullness of God's plans for our lives. Nobody wants these trials and tribulations to come, but it takes something special to see the good in everything. During my trials, I was able to survive by seeing the good in my situations. Even when we think there is no good, having in mind that God has great plans for His children is enough. Everyone knows what a compass is, right? The compass shows us directions. It is time to start seeing those *problems* you think you are facing as a compass that is directing you to the Promised Land. Generally, there is no glory without a story, in life and the bigger your story, the bigger the glory.

Do you know that as a child of God, you are already destined for greatness? God has a specific purpose for each and every person He created. Isaiah 44:24 reads, "Thus says the Lord, your Redeemer, who formed you from the womb; I am the Lord, who made all things, who alone stretched out the earth by myself." This bible verse goes to illustrate the magnanimity of the Lord. What I understand from this verse is that when God forms someone in their mother's womb, He has a specific purpose for you. You can be sure that this purpose is not to see you fail. Another bible verse that serves as an inspiration and source of hope for me during my trying times is Jeremiah 1:5. It reads, "Before I formed you in the womb I knew you, and before you were born I consecrated you; I appointed you a prophet to the nations." Any believer of the word of God should know how highly God rates his prophets. In the old times, prophets were those people who did the work of the Lord along with speaking it. They were revered, and God did whatever they asked of Him. We know of many prophets in the bible, both minor and major, and they all served God and demonstrated His might. However, since the crucifixion and death of our Lord Jesus Christ, every child of God has become a prophet. Well, let me explain what I mean by that.

Do you remember that there was a part of the temple that was consecrated that only prophets and priests were allowed in, in the Old Testament? The big curtain that separated God's people from the presence of God? When Jesus died on the cross, that curtain was torn from the top to the bottom. There may be many interpretations for that but what I can say is that it meant that there was no special person who needed to go to the presence of the Lord. We all have access now. The death of Jesus Christ made each and every Christian a prophet and priest in his or her own rights. So why think that God would allow His ordained prophets to fail? Now let's be clear, we are not all walking in the office of a prophet; but we all have the same access to the gift of prophecy because of the Holy Spirit and we are all a part of the royal priesthood since Jesus's death and resurrection. Why question the plans and purposes God has for His prophets?

Going through trials and tribulations is a very tricky phase of life. The reason I say this is because sometimes you may feel like giving up. The mind is one of the most powerful weapons in the fight for survival. It is so powerful that before you win or lose the fight in the physical, your mind must have already won or lost the fight. So during your struggles, you need to guard your mind and heart. In fact, it is clearly written in Proverbs 4:23. It reads, "Guard your mind above all else, for it determines the course of your life."

So if you want to come out stronger and better after all your trials and tribulations, guard your heart and mind. Condition your mind to believe that you are a survivor and that you are going to come out better and stronger. When the troubles become seemingly overwhelming, trust the mind to start trying to trick you into believing that you are already losing the battle. But believe me, when I say you are not losing the battle, you are actually growing! Yes, I said it. You are actually growing.

As a child of God, you do not have to survive hard times. Why? Because you are already a victor because Christ has already died for you. With that death came victory, and He has shared it with all of us. So for anyone reading this, you do not need to *survive* when you can live knowing that Christ already died for it and you. When those tough times come around, all you have to do is believe that you are simply experiencing a moment when God is planning to exercise your faith muscle and grow you into the next dimension. It takes a certain level of faith to believe that those *hard times* are actually preparing you for a greater purpose and success.

I like to use myself as a case study because I have been through a lot of things in my life, especially recently. The toughest phase of my life was when I was battling COVID-19 at the end of 2020. We are all aware of what the pandemic caused and how it negatively shaped the world in 2020. I was tested in different aspects: my ministry, finances, marriage, and even my health. You would notice that I did not use the phrase, "The devil was attacking me." I always believe that all trials and tribulations are forms of tests aimed at strengthening my faith. It was like my health, marriage, finances, and ministry were all taking a negative turn all at the same time. If you were in my shoes, what would you do?

Well, because I am here sharing my testimony, it could only mean one thing; I survived it and came out stronger. During those trying times, all I had to do was to see things differently from how a man without faith would. And let me tell you, it was a struggle at times. A real struggle. But I exercised my faith and begin to not see it as an attack from the enemy. Though at first, I was seriously inclined to thinking so. But eventually, I started getting the revelation from God that all those scary moments were actually moments that were preparing me for my growth and repentance. So instead of panicking and looking for ways to *survive* it, I saw those moments as moments for me to *thrive.* A saying goes, "Before a seed grows, it must be buried." That's scripture too. With this in mind, I started picturing myself in those times as being buried, with the hope that I will, one day, grow and blossom. By the grace of God, those times are over.

In moments of despair, it is up to you to activate your faith in God. That simple action will catapult you to greatness. Instead of surviving, start thriving. It will see you through whatever storm you may be going through.

How does one activate their faith in God?

Nobody said it was going to be easy to activate your faith during trying times. I say this because I have been there before and I am speaking from experience. But I want to share the simple way I was able to activate my faith in those trying times. If this worked for me, I believe it will work for you too. Because we're no different.

Get out of your own way.

Sometimes, we are the ones standing in the way of our own success. You have to let the Holy Spirit be your guide in everything you do as a true Christian. How exactly do you do this?

- You have to be able to differentiate between your carnal voice and the spiritual voice of God; and you must be willing to obey God's voice even if it's uncomfortable. Most times, we think we have heard the voice of the Lord. But what is the use of hearing His voice if you do not work according to what you heard? How can one operate spiritually and carnally at the same time? It's not possible. The bible says we are in the world, but not of the world. This simply means that even though we have flesh, we should not act according to it. Acting according to the flesh is the way people go astray. God is a spiritual being, and since He made us in His own image, we should to live accordingly.

- You must learn to walk in the spirit by walking in faith. Adam, for example, was the first man God created. The bible recorded that Adam used to commune with God as a son would his father. But what happened when he decided to walk according to his flesh? He lost that communion with God. This led to his banishment from the Garden of Eden and the beginning of suffering, trials, and tribulations for all mankind. It is just the same way with us. Some people actually started well with God, kept the faith, and were thriving under the direction of the Holy Spirit. But somewhere along the line, they lost it all and gave in to the demands of the flesh. God is holy and does not work according to the flesh. So once a believer begins to walk according to the flesh, they are cut off from the grace of God, and that is when the real trials and tribulations surface. Some say, "It is difficult to live a life of faith; try living a life without faith!" I would most certainly have to agree.

- Have you ever noticed that something inside of you tells you to try and retrace your steps whenever you are going astray? Yes, the Holy Spirit is in every believer and is ever-present to direct our footsteps. He is our compass, and sometimes the trials we face are our cardinal directions. Pointing us right where we need to go and where we need to be. Whenever we feel like we are not getting it right, it is very important to reassess our relationship and our success of hearing God. Being able to thrive in times of trials and tribulations is dependent on your stance with God. Someone who is not on the same frequency with God in the spirit cannot thrive in life's trials and temptations. When you access your faith and stance with God, you will then be able to know whatever it is that stands in the way between you and

God. Like they say, "Knowing your problem is solving half of the problem." The Holy Spirit walks with a Christian who is in line with what the spirit says. When Jesus was leaving the earth and ascending to heaven, He said in John 14:26 that He would send the Holy Spirit to teach us those things we may have forgotten.

- When I faced those hard times back in 2020, I almost gave up, but something came to my mind. I began to ask myself, "Is it because God sees greatness in me that He is allowing these tests to come my way so that I can manifest fully?" Using a general illustration, "Nobody throws stones at a tree without ripe fruits." You must begin to understand that the reason you are facing these hard times is that God is making sure that you are the best version of yourself when He is ready to give you your blessings. Some

41

people keep praying for God's blessing, and they refuse to understand that you need to be prepared for the blessings. The Lord will not just bless whoever He does not deem ready, and the best way to make you blessing-ready is to make sure you undergo those litmus tests and come out stronger, better, and wiser.

- We have to start believing that God does not start a project He will not finish. The fact that He has started to refine you by allowing your faith to be tested shows that He is just getting started with you. He is a loving father and does not just enjoy inflicting pain on us. He takes glory when the tests bring out the best He has embedded in you. In almost every area of life, your best comes out after you have put in the hard work. How you handle all of the tough situations you encounter in your life goes a long way. It determines your growth in the spirit and brings forth the manifestation of God's promises to you in your natural life.

- You must learn how to measure God's love. We've got to appreciate Him in whatever situation we find ourselves. One of the most popular verses in the bible, John 3:16, reads, "For God so loved the world that He gave His only begotten son." This does not even begin to measure the amount of love God has for us. But it does exemplify that He has a great love for us. In knowing this, we've got to know that this love does not mean we are not going to be tested. When an earthly father disciplines a child that goes astray, it does not mean He does not love His child. In fact, it is because of this love that He finds the time to try and correct the child. God sees the best in all of us as His children, and He always finds the time to call us back from our wrong paths, put us on the right track, and propel us to be what He created us to be. Through all these trials and temptations, we should understand that God is giving us an opportunity to be with Him at the next level.

In the next few chapters, let's talk about what you will need for your spiritual journey. We will be dissecting some spiritual angles and giving you a toolbox that you will need to not only survive through hard times, but thrive, come out better, and be a better version of yourself. It is of great importance that you see that it's not enough just to survive it, you must thrive in it.

Submission & Obedience

"Obedience is better than sacrifice!!!"

If you are a parent or an elder sibling and you give an instruction to a younger person to do something, but after a long day's journey, you come back to see that your instruction was not followed, how would you feel? Then imagine trying to stamp your authority on the person who disobeyed you, and they are not submissive... There will be a feeling of anger and maybe the urge to become violent for the average human being. This simply means that these two traits can be very annoying and frustrating, right?

So in order to be triumphant and survive hard times, you need to find the area of repentance. Repentance, in this context, would just mean the balance between submission and obedience. In the general Christian community, when someone goes astray and somewhere along the line, he or she decides to come back to God, become obedient to His word and submissive to His will, we can say that person has repented of all their sins.

Contrary to what most Christians believe, repentance does not necessarily mean that one has committed sins that are deadly and unforgivable. Even though you can repent from every sin, no matter how grievous or small the sin is, I want to view repentance as an opportunity to make amends in areas that you ought to do better. As I stated earlier, the Holy Spirit resides in every Christian, and one thing is sure, it gives us the direction toward the light. But what happens when a Christian strays from the right path? The Holy Spirit whispers the corrections into the mind of the Christian, and all the Christian has to do is... Repent! So repentance could just mean a slight or big adjustment on your path to righteousness.

Times of repentance can be known as "Kairos moments." What exactly are Kairos moments? These are moments or opportunities that allow for a shift, a new turn, or repentance. In the New Testament, kairos moments are described as the appointed time to do something, according to the plan and purpose of God. We can say kairos moments are generally the "Now Time." The time when God finally wants to do something in your life. If you look at a dictionary, Kairos moments are described in different terms, all pointing to the appointed time or moment. Kairos' moments are not measured by hours or minutes but by what is currently happening in your life. An unbeliever can be doing many bad things in their life and get away with them. But when it is time for a kairos moment, everything changes in the blink of an eye.

The bible said, in Romans 13:11, "And do this, understanding the present time; The hour has already come for you to wake up from your slumber because our salvation is nearer now than we first believed" This part of the bible felt like a shot of adrenalin during my trying times. Whenever I felt like giving up, I felt myself being activated by a kairos call from this verse of the bible. The Holy Spirit is ever-present in every situation and is moving to accomplish a purpose, according to God's plan and for His eternal glory.

Permit me to dissect the Kairos moment a little further. You need to understand that the Kairos moment is divided into three different stages. Yes, the Kairos moment happens in a flash sometimes, but it is a process made up of these three stages;

• First, the spirit of God starts moving over a particular situation. That situation could be anything like your time of need, your hard times, times you may be going contrary to the will of God, etc. Do you know that a true believer is naturally able to discern God's presence? Have you ever been in a situation where you felt like giving up, and somehow your faith gets boosted, and a sudden surge of hope starts to flow through your spiritual being? Yes, that is the presence of the Holy Spirit in your life, giving you all you need to survive and thrive through those difficult times. Some may have described this rush as a form of electricity flowing through the body or heat in their hand. Others may have described it as a strong word forming in their hearts and minds, and some others cannot even describe how they feel.

Whatever the case, having a convicted certainty in your mind or heart that God will see you through is all that you need.

• Second, we begin to get direction and guidance from the Holy Spirit. After discerning that the Holy Spirit is there to give you all the hope, comfort, and strength that you need, you need to stay calm and realize that the Holy Spirit will also give you directions and guidance on how to act according to the will of God. How one can get guidance from the Holy Spirit differs, but the common ways may just be through scripture in the bible, through going down on your knees to God in prayer, or some other means that may differ from individual to individual. What is important is receiving guidance from the Holy Spirit.

• Third, you now need to step out in submission and obedience. We are right back where we started; submission and obedience. First, you need to understand that without submission and obedience, guidance means little or nothing. In submission, we pray for direction, and in obedience, we follow what the Holy Spirit tells us. You don't need to assume anything on God's behalf. Many Christians are guilty of this, acting of their own volition and assuming it is God's direction they are following. Let us take King Saul as a case study; in 1 Samuel 13, Saul paid a heavy price for his disobedience to God. He was told to wait for Samuel to arrive before offering any sacrifice, but he decided to act of his own volition, and what was the result? God stripped the kingdom from him and his lineage forever.

After getting the direction, you need to "follow" it. That is the only way to complete the Kairos moment. God never leads His people astray, so once you hear the voice and follow it, you will survive anything that comes your way.

Careful observation would reveal that we have mentioned submission and obedience a couple of times. Let us take some time to understand what each one means. It will help to paint a better picture of what God wants from us.

What is submission?

According to the general dictionary meaning, submission is the act of yielding to a higher authority or accepting to do the will of that higher authority. For an average human being, it takes a whole lot for one to be submissive. Imagine being told to do something you do not want to do, but you have to do it anyway because the instruction is coming from a higher authority... It can be a really tough decision. But I can confidently tell you that the first step to being submissive is believing that the higher authority you are submissive to is acting in your best interests. As a child of God, you have to be submissive to the

I SURVIVED | THOMAS

will of God. His thoughts for us are thoughts of good always, so once a Christian understands that fact, submission begins to come naturally. If you do not trust your leader or a higher authority, it is logical not to be submissive because of the doubts in your mind. As Christians, we must learn to be submissive to things because we will definitely have absolute authority over them.

You need to have a deeper and better understanding of timing. You also need to understand that you cannot have absolute control over everything. Your control over things may take a little longer than you anticipated, and this is why you need to understand timing. Sometimes, it feels like you are being overcome, overpowered, or placed under the immense pressure, authority, or weight of something. Yes, it can really feel that way sometimes. In those situations, what do you do? Learn to bid your time and submit when necessary because, in due time, you will reign over that situation later. Most importantly, you need to always be submissive to the will of God. His ways are not our ways, so as long as you are sure you are on the right path, it does not matter the trials and tribulations that come your way, and you will always conquer.

Obedience to the will of God

Obedience is simply the willingness to comply with the order, commands, or requests of a higher authority. You cannot be obedient without being submissive and vice versa. They work hand in hand. However, obedience is the action itself. We can just say that being submissive is agreeing to the demands of a higher authority, while obedience is actually acting according to the will of the higher authority. As a Christian who understands the will of God, you cannot just go around submitting to any other power or authority.

That is the track path to cowardice. The Holy Spirit is there to instruct us on how to be submissive to the will of God.

The truth is, sometimes, we know who we need to be submissive to when the time arises. We will not always have our way, and that is a constant in life. Even as a true believer, things will not always go your way, and that is where the tests, trials, and tribulations come in. But when things happen contrary to what you have planned, you need to understand when to be submissive and when to stand your ground. If you need to be submissive, do so because it will help you grow up both spiritually and physically, and it will also teach you those things you may not have learned if things always went your way.

Take, for instance, a worker who is employed by a boss in an office. If the boss does not possess a good character, does that mean you need to quit your job? No, because the bible says, in Matthew 10:16, "Behold, I am sending you out as sheep in the midst of wolves; so be wise as serpents and innocent as doves." This verse is trying to explain something; First, Jesus acknowledges that it is not easy to be obedient and submissive in a world like ours, so we, as Christians, are sheep in the midst of wolves. The wolves may just be the tests, trials, and tribulations we face every day. Second, He is teaching us to be wise as serpents and innocent as doves. In our example, only a person who is not wise will leave his or her source of income because of the boss's character. Also, only someone who is not filled with the Holy Spirit will react in a negative way to all the trials and tests that come. So, in this kind of situation, you need to be gentle and innocent and apply wisdom in all you do. If the boss does not like something, don't do it. If he or she does not like being challenged, even though you may be right, be submissive and obedient. As we said before, being submissive and obedient will help you become a master of the situation someday. By the master of the situation, I mean that someday, you will become your own boss. All I am trying to say is that there are times to be obedient and submissive, and only the Holy Spirit will direct you on what to do, according to the will of God.

When you are obedient and submissive, you will understand that there will come a time and place to take full authority. Just like the example above, after serving, you will take full authority someday. When you are serving, God looks at how humble, obedient, and submissive you are. You are showing God that you are mature enough and ready to be elevated to the next stage of your life. And with a better understanding of timing, you will realize that all the while, God has been setting you up for something bigger. All the trials and tests were just to make sure that you are prepared for it. Jesus is a perfect embodiment of submission and obedience. He was submissive to the will of the Father even until death... Till the very end. I believe every Christian has to learn from that. To confirm what we said earlier, Jesus later had complete authority over death. While he was praying, in Matthew 26:39, he said, "o my Father, if it is possible, let this cup pass from me: nevertheless not as I will, but as thou wilt." I learned a lot of things from this verse. One, I was able to understand that as long as you are in the flesh, you may reach the point where you can no longer endure the pain. Jesus saw what he was going to pass through, and his flesh was afraid. He begged God to find him another way instead of the pain and trials he was going to face. At that point, the Holy Spirit was present to console and strengthen him. Two, even with all the fear of the pains and trials he was about to face, he still said, "Nevertheless not as I will, but as thou wilt." This is the ultimate example of total submission and obedience to the will of God. I have a question for you, if Jesus, our Lord, and personal savior, was totally submissive and obedient to the will of God, who are we to act of our own will?

While I was passing through my trials and temptations, I will not deny being stretched to the point where I felt I was going to give up and break. It felt like the world was turning against me. In fact, at some point, I thought I could not hear the voice of the Lord or follow His directions. Many of us may be in that kind of situation as you read, but there is good news; I was able to survive all that happened to me, and here I am, telling my story and trying to tell you that no mountain is too great for the Lord to move. He created everything, and only He has the power to change every situation and break every chain.

The importance of submission and obedience can never be emphasized. Abraham was made the Father of all nations because he was totally submissive and obedient to the will of God. So, remain submissive and obedient and see if God will not pull you out of whatever dire situation you may be in.

Vision

"Oh Lord, open my eyes that I may see what you have planned for me." Yes! That should be your everyday prayer point. If God opens your eyes to see what He has planned for you, you will become submissive and obedient. A man without vision cannot reach his goals. To survive through hard times, you need to have a mental picture of the plans and purpose for God in your life. That mental picture you are creating is your vision. The dictionary describes vision as the ability or sense of sight. In this spiritual context, we will be seeing vision as more than the ability to see. I want to see a vision as the goal toward which a Christian aspires or a supernatural encounter with God. When some people pray, they say, "Lord, open my eyes." That is a very valid prayer point because, without vision, you cannot work according to what God planned for you.

Without vision, you cannot walk in the faith. Vision is a tool for triumph in hard times. Take, for instance, a child can walk through a lonely place once he or she can see, but in times of darkness, that same child becomes afraid to step out on their own. This simply highlights the importance of vision. The same principle applies to us as Christians. If we cannot see where we are going, then how do we get there? It is important to see and know what is going on around you, both spiritually and physically, for you to be able to make it through those dark seasons of your life. Without vision, it is almost impossible to triumph.

I say this because when someone is placed in a dark place or situation, the first instinct is to be afraid. Now, this is normal considering the fact that we are humans and are made of the flesh. But for a true believer, God's vision should always be with you always. Panic is a tool that has been known to hamper the success of people who were destined to be great. I, for instance, went through things that would have made many people panic. Having issues and challenges with almost every aspect of my life was not easy for me. Everywhere I turned, problems and challenges seemed to be waiting for me. But by the special grace of God, I did not panic. Why? Because I was able to see the plans God has for me. Remaining calm and collected was the way I survived through the storm. If you are able to see in the dark, there is no way fear will overtake you. In the movies, we can see that soldiers who had night vision goggles always had advantages over the enemies that did not. The same rule applies; when you are in a very dark place, trust God to give you the night vision you need to see that there is always light at the end of the tunnel. If you think the problems are weighing down on you, take some time to calm and collect yourself, draw inspiration and motivation from the fact that God is by your side and the Holy Spirit is leading the way. With these thoughts come maximum comfort and the strength to not only survive but thrive through these trying times.

One good example of God's vision is illustrated in 2 Kings. Elisha was a great prophet who carried out wonderful assignments for God. If you read the full chapter, the King of Syria sought to do Elisha harm before attacking the people of Israel. He called his servants and asked them who the Prophet was and how to get him. They told him, and he sent a full army to Dothan, where Prophet Elisha was at the time. There are some illustrations I need to point out from this part of the bible;

• One, the servant of the Man of God, observed the surroundings, saw a large host of army, and his first instinct was to panic. We have talked about how panic is the first thing people do when they encounter a trial or test. The bible recorded that he ran to his master and asked what could be done.

• Two, Prophet Elisha, being a man of God and filled with the Holy Spirit, was so calm about the "situation" they were in. I want to believe that the servant had a hard time comprehending why his master was so calm in this situation. The Prophet replied, "Fear not; for they that be with us are more than they that be with them." The servant must have wondered again what his master was talking about. I was in a similar situation while I was going through my struggles. I kept hanging onto the promises and vision of God, but people around me thought I had lost my mind. Imagine trying to stay calm when the world seemed to be crumbling around you!!!

• Three, the spiritual vision. Prophet Elisha already had the vision, but he wanted his servant to witness the awesomeness of the God he was serving. So he said a simple prayer, "Lord, I pray thee, open his eyes that he may see." When God opened the servant's eyes, the vision was breath-taking. The mountain was surrounded by horses and chariots of fire. The servant instantly believed that the Prophet Elisha was serving a living God.

• Four, without sight, there is no direction. Still, in the same chapter and book of the bible, when the earthly host of the Syrian army began to descend on Prophet Elisha and his servant, he asked God to strike them with blindness. As a child of God, you need to understand that God is capable and willing to grant your every request, as long as it is in line with His principles. God struck them with blindness, and something else happened. Because they were blind, they could not reach their goal. Prophet Elisha led them to another place entirely. If they were not blind, they would have known who was talking to them and would have done what they were supposed to do. He led them to Samaria, where the army of Israel was waiting, and they were just like sheep led to the slaughter. That is how a Christian is without a vision; sheep led to the slaughter.

There are two types of vision a Christian needs to be able to walk with God. I will be discussing both of them, and one does not go without the other.

• The first type of vision is the practical vision: The practical vision can be seen as the visualization of that natural result that God wants to happen in your physical life as a result of your current trials and tribulations. First, you need to understand that there is a reason for everything. God, who planned, designed, and created the universe, is the ultimate architect. So when you are going through trying times, you need to understand that God has a reason for that. You may want to work in an office for some reason. But maybe God has a better plan for you even though you do not see it. You think you know what is best for yourself, but trust me, God knows what is best for everyone. As His children, we are His priorities. So if you face some difficulties getting into that office, it could be a way God is using to direct you to maybe try a career path that may be more successful for you. God may want you to become a businessman, so you will be able to travel around the world, meet more people, and in the end, be able to win more souls. This is just an example; all I am trying to say is whenever physical things are not going the way you plan, you need a practical vision to be able to see and understand God's plan for you in the physical world.

- The second type of vision is the spiritual vision: The spiritual vision can be described as the visualization of the spiritual result God wants to get from you as a result of your trials, tests, and tribulations. Are you a person of little faith? Maybe God wants to use your current test to strengthen your faith. Are you backsliding? Maybe God wants to use your present test to draw you closer to Him. Sometimes, we go through trying times so that the name of the Lord may be glorified. All it needs is a spiritual eye and vision to understand that everything happens for a reason. God is always preparing us for something better because He is our loving father. So that spiritual character that is trying to lead you away from the faith can be overcome through tests, trials, and tribulations. All you need to do is have the vision.

These two types of vision are necessary for the life of a Christian. The practical and spiritual vision work hand in hand to help Christians visualize what God believes is best for them. Remember that these types of vision are related to the physical eyes. In fact, let us stress this point a little. Without vision, generally, it is impossible to succeed in your plans. Do you want to go to work? You need eyes to see where you are going. Do you want to do anything? You need eyes to see what it is you want to do. The same applies to the practical and spiritual vision. I believe God gives us those types of vision so that we can be in line with his plans and purposes for our lives. Also, you do not need to assume anything on God's behalf. Be sure you have the right vision from God and act accordingly.

Lastly, you need not be anxious about anything. As we agreed, there is absolutely no need to act on God's behalf. Are you having a really bad time in your life? Are the trials and tribulations becoming too much for you to bear? Do you think it is the right time for God to act? Philippians 4:6 reads, "Do not be anxious about anything, but in every situation, by prayer and petition, with thanksgiving, present your requests to God." Whatever it is anyone is going through, as long as you are a child of God, this verse is for you. You need to keep calm and let God fight your battles. Some people mistake being calm for doing nothing. They are not the same thing. In those hard times, children of God should go down on their knees and pray, fast, give thanks and continue what they are doing. If a Christian is going through problems in their marital life, would you want them to do nothing just because they are staying calm? No. The first step would be to go to the Lord in prayer. But it does not stop the Christian from trying physical ways to save their relationships. Visits can still be made to a marriage counsellor; they can always try to work things out between them through dialogues and dates, and so on. So when the Lord tells you to keep calm, it does not mean you do not need to make conscious efforts. But as we have said before, you should not act on God's behalf while trying to make conscious efforts.

Also, 1 Peter 5:7 reads, "Cast all your anxiety on Him because he cares for you." This verse goes to show us that the Lord is aware of our tendency to be anxious. He is our creator, and He knows our capabilities. What He wants us to do is cast our burdens on Him whenever we feel anxious. This simply means that being anxious is not bad; it's what you do in those anxious times that matter.

"When you have done everything you can do, that's when God will step in and do what you can't do" - 2 Corinthians 12:10. This was one of my most inspirational verses during those difficult times I had. I knew I had done everything I could to save myself from all the trials and tribulations I was enduring at the time. At one point, I had to just kneel and tell God to take the wheel. At that point, I realized that I could do nothing more, and that was when God stepped in, turned the situation around, and made me a survivor. Do the same when you are at your breaking point, and watch God turn

you into a success story.

4

Movement Coordination

"Have I not commanded you? Be strong and courageous. Don not be frightened, and do not be dismayed, for the Lord your God is with you wherever you go." - Joshua 1:9

"Wherever you go." The Lord is going with you. One important tool for getting through hard times is movement coordination. In fact, our biology classes tell us that movement is one of the essentials of every living thing. Well, in this context, we will be discussing and addressing movements more as decisions because we are dealing with things of the spirit.

First, what does the dictionary describe the movement as? It says the movement is the physical motion between two points. So if you leave a spot to another spot, you have been deemed to have moved. But the chapter reads, "Movement coordination" so we need to address coordination too. Coordination can be seen as the act of making different things work together to achieve a common goal. With the idea of these two, we can say that movement coordination is the motion between places that are in line with a common goal. I hope I got this right, but this is just the physical aspect of it.

Do you know that whatever moves or decisions you make are sure to affect the generation after you? Just like we descended from earlier generations, people will also descend from us. And what you do today will determine how your next generation would be. We have been talking about survival all this while, so let me tell you something. If you are not spiritually strong enough to survive what life throws at you, your generation will be made to suffer whatever the outcome of your spiritual failure. As children of the next generation, some things are not taught in schools and churches, but of course, you knew that already. The most basic type of education is the one the children get at home. For instance, a child does not learn how to pray in the school or church. He or she would learn it naturally as long as they have prayerful parents. When they wake up in the morning, and the first thing they see their parents do is go down on their knees in prayer to their heavenly Father, the children will have to do the same. The bible says in Proverbs 22:6, "Train up a child in the way he should go, and when he is old, he will not depart from it."

Contrary to what most people believe, children can be very observant. In fact, that is the natural way they learn things in life. My son is a perfect example. As I said before,

I SURVIVED | THOMAS

at one point in my life, I was going through a lot of trials and tribulations. My son was there beside me, and I knew he was watching my every move. He watched in silence, and I believe he must have learned a few things from my experiences.

Right before I started to experience a lot of problems in my life, I had announced to my congregation that my biological son would succeed me as the new pastor of the church. This is a church I have headed for years, but I had my doubts about the transition, if I am truly honest. These doubts did not come from doubting my son's abilities because I knew my son was equal to the task. I believe it may have come from my comfortability. What do I mean? As a leader, I had held on to my position as the head of the church for so many years that it felt natural that I would be the head. I thought I had mastered the position, had a lot of spiritual experience, and had believed that nobody would do it better.

I think I was too complacent that I forgot that leading God's people is a task assigned to people. I was assigned the task, but I did not want to believe that my job was done. So I held on to the position longer than ordained by God. In a way, I believe that my trials and tribulations were made to just shake me out of that position in obedience to God's will. I may have been guilty of thinking or acting on God's behalf because I felt like I was the best man for the job, so the trials may have come to nudge me towards God's plan for me.

So every move I made in those critical times was observed by my son. I know I am a human, but God helped me not to make the wrong moves. My movement coordination was ordered by the Almighty, and I believe my son noticed it because if I had made the wrong moves, I am convinced that I would have been passing the wrong legacy to him. I kept praying to God to help me make the right moves, both for myself and for the son I was passing my legacy to. It all boils down to what I mentioned earlier; the generation after you learns from your actions. I kept reminding God that he is the one that chose me, and he should not allow me to make the wrong moves. I believe my son was praying just as much as he was watching because he would not have liked to inherit an unhealthy legacy. Being a man of God, he was also prayerful, vigilant, observant, and wanted to walk in the right direction.

Whenever you do anything, you need to realize that you are setting up the next generation for failure if you do not survive your own test. In Deuteronomy 4:9-10, the bible says, "But watch out! Be careful never to forget what you yourself have seen. Do not let these memories escape from your mind as long as you live! And be sure to pass them on to your children and grandchildren, Never forget the day when you stood before the Lord your God at Mount Sinai, where he told me, Summon the people before me, and I will personally instruct them. Then they will learn to fear me as long as they live, and they will teach their children to fear me also." Please do me a favour, and read this passage again. That part recognizes two facts;

• That we will go through some challenges in our lives, it says, "Do not let these memories escape from your mind as long as you live." There will always be trying times you would rather want to forget. That is a fact. However, you need to remember those times for one reason.

• So that you can teach them to your children and grandchildren. In my case, I believe I was able to teach my son a lot of things without even having to sit him down and talk to him. With God's help, I survived all the trials and tribulations that came my way at that point in time.

Obviously, my son was learning something from me. He must have learned to always worship the God his Father worshipped because he saw the great hand of God in my life and situation. The bible has always mentioned where fathers have thought their children to worship the God they worshipped. Abraham thought Isaac to worship God, and Isaac, in turn, thought Jacob to do the same. There are other instances in the bible where people decided to worship the God of their Father because of His wondrous works. It would be a thing of joy to know that my son learned to worship the God I worship and pass the same principle down to his children. In the same vein, anyone reading this book should always bear in mind that how you handle your current life challenges would likely be how your children would handle them. If you handle it with God's direction and total obedience and submission to His will, your children will do the same.

When you are in a struggle of your own, have you sat down to ask yourself this question, am I passing a legacy because of wrong motives, or am I doing so with a healthy heart? Well, let me break it down further. Some parents do some things just because their children are watching them. They do not even do those things because of the spiritual and physical implications. The wrong motives are just numerous. I still want to use myself as a case study. If I had done what I did just because I wanted to impress my son, I might have gotten it all wrong. I may even have failed God, myself, and my son in the process. So I can say everything I was doing in that period was out of the pureness of my heart. I was making the right decisions and passing along the right cues to the generation that was watching in a very healthy way. At some point, I did not even recognize that my son was watching because I was so focused on what God wanted me to do and how to get out of my problems. However, as the younger generation, my son and other members of the church were always watching me.

The fascinating thing about the next generation is that they may not necessarily be your biological children. You can keep saying that you want to make the path straight for your biological children, but what of those other children who look up to you as an inspiration? What do you call them? They are also called the next generation. In my case, heading a church means that all the young children in my church are the young generation. In your workplace, the people you supervise can be seen as your next generation. Supervisors are supposed to be older and more experienced than the next generation. It is your responsibility as a supervisor to lead the next generation aright with a healthy heart. The interesting thing is, no matter who you are and what role you play, there is always someone who looks up to you. The younger generation looks up to you and learns how to maneuver through the storms of life. Are you doing it the right way? Either way, you are teaching someone something. They are closely watching to see how you survive the situation.

I have a pastor friend whose name is Pastor Michael Benton of Fairfield Baptist Church. He told me that, "People have asked me why I am retiring so soon?" He said to me, "I wanted to land this airplane while I had plenty of runway."

Many pastors in the world today do not give enough time for the next generation to safely and effectively make their transition into power. They stay in their roles a little too long. I want to tell you that nobody stays in a position forever. Even Moses, who led the people of God out of Egypt, was not the one who led them to the Promised Land. God appoints everyone for a given time, and when it is time to pass the torch, it is always better to do it peacefully. Why stay longer than you need to when you can always groom the next generation to continue the Lord's work.

Well, in my opinion, one of the reasons for those trying times of mine may have been to remind me that my time was up. I have served God diligently all my life, and for some reason, I did not think I needed to pass the torch to anyone else. However, the dark times reminded me that I needed to move on. As a pastor of my local church, I was used to being the head of everything. Everything went through me, and I was God's instrument. However, I felt it was time to move to something greater.

International ministry seemed to be my next level for me. I needed to move from my local church and propagate the gospel to the world. I also needed to be sure my son knew how to take off on his own runway of leadership. I could not do that if I became old and incapable. So I had to pass the torch when I was capable and make sure to guide him on the path to greatness. I realized deep within me that I needed to land my plane locally. By landing my plane locally, I mean I needed to end my local ministry. Locally, I felt I was done, and my trials and tests at that time went a long way to stress that point. The next best thing I knew God wanted for me was to move my ministry internationally. I will still serve serve as Oveseer of the local church. This will give my son the support that he needs, and it will give our congregation the peace of knowing that I still support them and my son as they move forward.

I always wanted to propagate the gospel far and wide, go to different places, share the word, win souls, and become an ambassador for Christ. I would not do that if I still remained the head of my local church. Some people may have wondered, isn't it still possible to do all these while still heading your local church? Well, it may have been possible, but I also may have been distracted by the running of the local church. I can confidently say that I felt comfortable knowing I was leaving the local church and the Lord's sheep in the hands of my capable son. God is a master planner, and I know that before He started to give me signs to leave the local church, He had already anointed a successor in my place. So I wanted to go international and leave my son, whom God ordained, to set up and establish his ministry, under my guidance, in the local church. The day I chose to announce that I was stepping aside for my son was one of the proudest and happiest days of my life. This was because I was happy to finally pursue my dreams of going international and also seeing my son start his path to greatness. I believe I was able to teach him a few things with my life and character, knowing he was watching me survive all the trials and temptations that came my way.

In my years as a minister, I was able to understand that the ministry of God was much more than preaching on a Sunday. Most Christians believe that Christianity is all about going to church on Sunday, listening to the sermon, coming back home, and moving on with their lives. Ministry is what we do for God's glory. It is based on where He placed us, the gifts He has given us, and what He has called us to do according to His wisdom and also for the propagation of the gospel. Ministry is all about giving ourselves, our talents, and our resources to serve the Lord and bless others in the process.

The idea that serving God or ministering has to do only with going to church, singing, reading the bible, and the like is not the right idea. According to Martin Luther, the ministry is much more than work done by pastors. In fact, the ministry has to do more with caring for people in their times of need. The leaders of the church should not be the only ones to be called ministers.

So I have confirmed that the tough season of my life was a confirmation that I needed to land that plane of local ministry and board the plane of international ministry. I believe God wants me to move to the next dimension, and He has shown me the signs through the trials and tests I survived. However, I am always grateful that I had the vision, both practical and physical, to see the ultimate plan of God for my life. Now, I know that I am meant for something greater, which is the international ministry, and the local church has found its new shepherd in my son. With God's help, the church would reach its promised land through him, and he too can pass the torch and teachings of the Lord to the younger generation.

5

Unload & Unpack

The younger generation wants to see the real deal. The real deal, in this context, would be that the younger generation wants to see God at work. They want to see real miracles. By the way, let us talk a little about miracles.

What are miracles, and how do they work? First, I need to let you know that only you can decide what a miracle is. However, generally, an unexplainable event that triggers the curiosity of humans and somehow inspires their awe is deemed as miraculous. Dictionaries describe miracles generally as an extraordinary event that manifests the divine intervention of God in human affairs. Some people do not believe in miracles because they do not believe in the existence of God. However, as a child of God, you should believe that miracles happen, and only God makes them happen.

Real moves of God are evident in different parts of the bible. Some biblical miracles are dramatic, while others are quiet. However, what they have in common is evidence of divine intervention. As long as one trusts God, miracles are bound to happen. Let me share two miracles that fascinate me the most in the bible.

In the book of Daniel 6, a story was recorded about how King Darius had Daniel, a prophet of God, thrown into the lions' den for not worshipping their false gods. To cut a long story short, King Darius returned to the den the next day to find that Daniel, a servant of God, was unharmed. In verse 22, Daniel said, "My God sent His angel, and He shut the mouths of the lions." Read verse 23, and you will discover that God sent his angel to perform that miracle because Daniel trusted and believed in God. Another fascinating miracle that has even been doubted by non-bible scholars is the feeding of five thousand people with five loaves of bread and two fish. The gospel books of the New Testament describe how Jesus used five loaves of bread and two fish. The food was meant for a little boy, but he trusted Jesus with his meal, and Jesus used it to feed the hungry crowd, and they were enough left-over.

The truth is if we believe in miracles, we will understand what messages and plans God has for us. I believe that each miraculous event that happens in our lives has something to teach us, just like I believe that God made me survive all my trials and tribulations to set me on a higher path and give me a higher purpose. No single explanation can fully describe the miracles we, as children of God, experience. But, in order for the younger generation to see and understand what miracles and plans God has for them, we, the current generation, have to seize our dark moments as times to reflect on how to unload and unpack our baggage from the plane God may be calling us to land after all.

This means that as the current generation, we need to take inventory of our legacy and the mantles we currently carry, and what we are passing down to them.

By taking inventory of our legacy, we need to know what we have done and what we need the younger generation to learn. Being called of God is a good thing, but have you ever thought of how it may feel when you are called of God, and you get a mantle from a spiritual father? There is nothing like it. Let me take you to a part in the bible that illustrates this; Elijah was a prophet of God, and Elisha was his servant. In 2 Kings 2:8-14, you will understand that Elijah was supposed to be taken up to heaven on that day. But Elisha followed him diligently, watching him closely, just like the younger generation is watching us, the current generation. In verse 8, it reads, "And Elijah took his mantle, and wrapped it together, and smote the waters, and they were divided hither and thither, so that they two went over on dry ground." In this context, we can see that Elijah can be classified as the current generation. When Elijah was to be taken up to heaven, he told Elisha, "Ask what I shall do for thee, before I be taken away from thee." He asked this question in verse 9, and Elisha answered, "I pray thee, let a double portion of thy spirit be upon me." Elisha got a double portion of the spirit because he saw Elijah go up into heaven in a chariot of fire. However, he had been handed a double portion of the mantle. In verse 14 of the same chapter, when he got back to the bank of river Jordan, he took Elijah's mantle and smote the waters saying, "Where is the Lord God of Elijah?" The river parted just like Elijah had parted it while they were going. So even though Elisha was called of God, but receiving a mantle from his spiritual father, Elijah, he received a double portion and became stronger in the spirit. This goes to show that there is a spiritual inheritance for every child of God, especially those of us who are true believers. However, we need to understand that God has already set a date for a transition in the life of every spiritual leader. Elijah held the mantle of God for years, and when it was time to go, he had to pass the mantle to Elisha, his spiritual successor, at the appointed time. People will come after us, and it is our duty to make sure that this transition is smooth and will come with no sorrow. Are you a spiritual leader that thinks you can lead God's people forever? Do you see signs to pass the mantle of leadership to the next generation? It just may be God calling you to perform a higher function. As a spiritual leader, it is your duty to always listen and obey the voice of the Lord.

While I was going through those troubles, trials, and tribulations, one thing was sure; I kept looking unto God to help me. I battled with a lot of problems. My health, finances, marriage, and even my ministry were facing challenges at the same time. It was like the whole world was against me. But then I thought of something; why am I a minister if I do not believe in the ministry of our Lord, Jesus Christ? The truth is the ministry of God brought me healing and gave me the strength to survive those difficult times. Whenever I thought of giving up, I reflected on the type of legacy I was going to leave for the younger generation. Knowing that they looked up to me was one reason I asked God to give me the strength to carry on. I was really scared of leaving them a wrong legacy. To the glory of God, I did not. So, what does it mean to unpack and unload?

As a Christian, I can confidently say that nobody is perfect. In fact, while praying, we always need to ask God for forgiveness, no matter how holy we think we are. There arc sins and burdens we carry with us, whether we choose to admit them or not. Now, when you want to pass the torch down to the younger generation, you need to do two types of unloading and unpacking. The first type of unloading and unpacking would be ridding yourself of all those sins and burdens you carry. If men of God face challenges, then anybody can. So how does one pass the mantle if there are still burdens of sin in one's life? Unpack and unburden yourself. Then, you will now be ready to pass the torch or mantle to the younger generation.

The second type of unpacking and unloading would be giving the younger generation all they need to succeed. The children of God are like sheep, and the man of God is like the shepherd. You need to understand that when it is time to move to a higher plane, the younger generation needs to be equipped for the task ahead. Just like Elijah equipped Elisha, it is up to every man of God to equip the next generation. The same thing applies in our everyday life. In a Christian household, the father of the house has to equip his son for the task of running the family and serving God as diligently as he has. The mother has to equip her daughter for the task of supporting a family, both spiritually and physically. I know I did my best to equip my son for the task of running the local ministry with both my words and my actions.

My father was a great man of God. As a prophetic, deliverance, and healing minister, he did not joke with the things of God. Every day, he prayed to God to give him the strength to serve Him better. However, he believed he was anointed for the national ministry. He headed the local church with all diligence and obedience to the will of God. He was able to win and save souls to the glory of God. But one day, he called me and said to me, "I can only teach you the prophetic, healing, and deliverance ministry for the national church." Initially, I did not fully understand what he meant, but after some time, it became clearer to me, especially when it was time for me to go into the international ministry. He did not give me anything for that because, according to him, he was cut out for the national ministry. I must confess that even though he did not give me the mantle for the international ministry, all I have learnt about the ministry of God came from him. He was the one that guided me through the path to serving God, and whatever I want to use for my international ministry was bestowed on me by God through him. As part of the younger generation, I watched and observed closely what my father was doing. Even in his own trying times, I could see that he was upright and stood his ground on the promise of God. I really witnessed a great man of God walk his life out in faith.

While I was in faraway Jamaica, my father passed away. He was the one who instructed me to go and minister in Jamaica, and I was so heartbroken when he passed. Surprisingly, he held on to the end of the crusade there. He was always urging me to go international with my ministry, and I obliged. While I was there in Jamaica, I received word that his condition was getting from bad to worse. They also said that they did not know how long he was going to stay. I kept wondering what I would do, and somehow it wanted to interfere with my ministry there in Jamaica. I kept receiving calls from my wife and family members to come back home. I knew I had to finish the Lord's work there in Jamaica, and it felt like my father knew also. I say so because it felt like he lived right until I finished my last sermon in Jamaica. It was just like he was watching and urging me on from his sickbed, as the one who admonished that I do not miss the opportunity to kick start my international ministry.

About a week prior to leaving for Jamaica, I was anointed by my international spiritual father. The way I see it, I was covered on all sides. I had the anointing and blessing of my international spiritual father and also the blessing and anointing of my local spiritual and biological father. After being anointed by my international spiritual father, I knew I was ready for the international ministry. At the point of my biological father's death, I realized that it was like he was not going to leave until I finished my first international assignment. It felt like he needed to be sure I was completely covered before he passed on. I would say I am very lucky to have my "two fathers in the Lord" looking out for me and supporting me at every turn. However, during my darkest hours in 2020, all these thoughts and experiences came back to me. I started to realize that the mantle of leadership was not an easy one to carry. I finally understood what it felt like to be covered. I was covered all-around earlier in my ministry, but at the time of my trials and tribulations, I knew my fathers were not there, so I had to look up to God. I had to pull on the mantle of grace and authority that my fathers gave me back then. It was not an easy task, but I knew I had to do something to survive the storm.

As a child of God, you need to understand that when dark seasons come, it is an indication that you have been predestined and ordained. It is always good to keep your eyes on the prize rather than on the distractions that may be looming nearby. I cannot get tired of emphasizing the fact that trials and tribulations must come; in fact, for a true child of God, they are inevitable. But what you need to understand is that as long as you have God by your side, you can survive any and every storm. Talking about storms, let us visit the bible as it is our book of faith.

Peter was a disciple of Jesus. We know the popular story of how Peter walked on water. But there is something I want us to learn from that story. In Matthew 14:22, Jesus made his disciples get into a boat and go ahead of him because he wanted to be by himself and pray on the mountainside. In verse 25, it reads, "Shortly before dawn, Jesus went out to them, walking on the lake." His disciples thought they have seen a ghost and were greatly terrified. But in verse 27, it reads, "But Jesus immediately said to them: Take courage! It is I. Do not be afraid." Peter wanted to be sure it was Jesus, so he said in verse 28, "Lord, if it is you, tell me to come to you on the water." Jesus commanded him to come, and Peter got out of the boat and began to walk on water. He did so for a considerable distance until... Fear overcame him. Immediately he took his eyes off Jesus and looked at his surroundings; off went his faith. He became afraid.

That is just what happens in the life of a Christian during trying times. When you are in the middle of a turbulent sea, you need to look up to God and not up to a man. As Jesus said to Peter, do not be afraid, for fear will make you become overwhelmed by your present problems. I was challenged from almost every aspect of my life in the year 2020, but I kept my eye on Jesus, just as Peter did before he gave in to fear. Jesus said in verse 31, "You of little faith, why did you doubt?" This goes to show that doubt leads to fear, and fear leads to loss of faith. I gained strength and courage from prayers during those difficult times.

I must admit, going through that storm was not easy at all. I had to fight with a lot of things. In fact, at some point, I lost sight of God's promises. This was because I felt everything was too much for me. Going through financial struggles, marital challenges, and issues with my ministry really took a toll on me. Sometimes, I would kneel down and lose the urge, zeal, and strength to pray. At some point, I began to ask God why I, and I know that was where I got it all wrong. Only someone who has lost faith in the process should ask that question. I had to ask God to forgive me because I knew in that instant that I had lost sight, and it took a lot of grace to bring me back on track, and I am grateful to God I survived.

Let The Healing Begin

"But he was wounded for our transgressions, he was bruised for our iniquities, the chastisement of our peace was upon him and by his stripes we are healed" – Isaiah 53:5.

When a human being has an injury or wound, the doctors treat the person, and most say, "Give it time to heal." This shows that healing is a gradual process that may take some time. Healing is the process where the body cells regenerate and repair themselves. The interesting thing is healing can be both physical and spiritual, and I know I my heart that the

Bible was not only talking about physical healing. I was also talking about spiritual healing. Physical healing has to do with the regeneration of the body cells, but that is not our main focus. Our focus is on spiritual healing. In Isaiah 53:5, it says, "and by his stripes, we are healed," and I know in my heart that the Bible was not talking about physical healing. It was talking about spiritual healing.

Have you been wounded by rejection, loss, betrayal, sins, trials, or temptation? Are the wounds still fresh and open and need healing? Just like physical wounds can leave you in pain and discomfort, spiritual wounds can leave your soul craving for peace, comfort, and wholeness. Even though the verse from Isaiah is mainly directed towards spiritual healing, we can also use it in the physical context. People pray for spiritual healing using this context and verse. But we have to believe that God is the ultimate physician, healing the body, soul, and spirit alike. The healing work of the stripes of Jesus means that we have become dead to sin and alive to righteousness. When we accept Jesus into our lives, any spiritual wounds we may be having begin to undergo the spiritual healing process. There are three major ways we get healed by the stripes of Jesus, and I will be discussing them shortly;

We are healed because Jesus suffered just like we did: The New Testament contains stories of the immense suffering of Jesus before and during the crucifixion. As children, many of us heard the stories and wondered why people were so violent and wicked. Now we are all grown up, and we realize that Jesus did it, so we do not have to go through such. That is one of the reasons he had stripes. While I was going through those trials and tribulations, I asked myself, who better to understand what I am going through than Jesus, who suffered and died on the cross for me? In Psalms 34, the Bible says that God is there for the broken-hearted and saves those who are crushed in spirit. At those trying times of my life, I admit that I was crushed in the spirit. Jesus felt so downcast that he asked why his father had forsaken him. My point is no matter the amount of suffering, trials, and tribulations you face, the Lord knows and understands. He is also near to console you. After all, in Isaiah 41: 10, God said, "Fear not, for I am with you.... I will strengthen you, I will help you."

We are healed of the wounds inflicted by our sins through the salvation of the cross: Some Christians suffer from this syndrome; they may have been forgiven for any crimes they may have committed, but somehow they seem to bear the guilt of those sins. Hanging onto past sins committed may lead to regrets and may lead to a slower healing process spiritually. Some even go on to ask this disheartening question, how can God forgive me when I cannot even forgive myself? Guilt can come in two forms;

Condemnation and Conviction.

Condemnation is what enemies use to prevent us from being spiritually healed totally. It is a way the enemy uses to torture us for the past. We need to let go and allow spiritual healing to take place. Condemnation can even be seen as a symptom of our inability to forgive ourselves. In Matthew 18:23, Jesus uses a parable to illustrate the importance of forgiveness, so we need to learn how to forgive.

Conviction is when the Holy Spirit gently corrects a Christian and restores them to their former glory. No sin is too great.

We are healed because we are spiritually whole in Christ Jesus: Now, we have been freed of condemnation and conviction. Jesus has comforted us because He suffered like us. We have been saved through the salvation of the cross. However, we need to be made whole by Christ Jesus. After healing blind Bartimaeus, Jesus said to him in Mark 10:52, "Go thy way; thy faith hath made thee whole." So receiving your healing is one part; you need to be made whole in Christ Jesus.

We all need healing in different forms; it may be in the form of a broken relationship, ministerial struggles, financial hardship, health challenges, broken dreams and promises, different types of guilt. The bottom line is Jesus can heal every kind of wound. I believe Jesus had all of us in His heart when He was going through all the troubles. So go to God, no matter the torments your soul is experiencing. God has already forgiven you, and Jesus has paid your debt in full.

Let us zone in on the marital aspect. We need to spend some time discussing marriage. Marriage is something that was ordained by God. Marriage is a culturally accepted and recognized union between two people of the opposite sex, called spouses or marriage partners, that establishes obligations and rights between them, their offspring, and in-laws. It is culturally universal. People marry for reasons like social, legal, emotional, financial, religious, and spiritual purposes. Their choice of partners is also influenced by some of these factors, and more factors like rules of interest, marital rules, individual desire, and maybe parental choice.

Coming back to my marital life, I still believe that God was trying to get me to understand that the number one reason for marriage is for ministry. As I said earlier, people marry for a number of reasons. Yes, they do. Mine was for the ministry. Let me describe what I mean.

Growing in love and togetherness in marriage is a great way to nurture your love for others, and most especially God. An intimate and vibrant marriage will help you become a more effective minister and a loving and supporting spouse.

Ministry is a high spiritual calling, and most ministers have busy agendas. Before now, pastors spent more time caring for their spiritual sheep and less time taking care of their wives and other duties at home. But as the years go by, we have witnessed many bad consequences of putting the ministry between a pastor and their family. I believe God wanted me to understand that saving my marriage would help my ministry. Today, many ministerial marriages encounter insidious and severe threats. This has led to the divorce of a lot of ministers with their wives. As a ministerial couple, we were not able to press "Pause" and take some time to reconnect, discuss our priorities, and find ways to balance my ministry and my marital relationship. We need to understand that God made marriage a "One-flesh" ideal, and he intended for us to enjoy it. We also need to note and discover God's ministry's relational, emotional, and spiritual impact on our marriages.

The time spent in building a loving, healthy, and happy relationship in marriage is so important to develop a very healthy and loving relationship with God. I see marriage as the "discovery center" for exploring the wonders of the love of God. In fact, the more we learn about intimate, deep, and committed love, the more we learn to understand that God loves us dearly. As we learn to love and protect our partners with all our soul, mind, strength, and heart, we also learn what it means to serve God with everything in us. And the more we love and serve God with all that is in us, the better our love for our partners and each other. We should learn to anticipate the relational needs of our partners in unselfish ways because this will help us understand better why God tirelessly caters for all our needs.

Accepting another person's support and care will teach us that we cannot do everything on our own, and we were not even meant to, or God would not have given us partners.

It will also help us to develop trust and humility in God. Protecting our partners from sadness, anger, pain, or worse will also teach us transferrable skills that can be applied to our ministry of love. When we appreciate the little or great things our partners do for us, we can learn to be grateful and appreciate the different ways God showers His love on us. Also, by making sacrifices to appreciate, support, love, comfort, or encourage our partners, we will get a feel of what Jesus sacrificed for us as our Lord and personal saviour.

We should also understand that we become better at working together with God to help us experience a deeper and richer relationship with Him through love.

In the beginning, Adam lived alone in the Garden of Eden and walked the face of the earth with God. God, having the interest of His son at heart, knew something was missing. In Genesis 2:18, the Bible reads, "And the Lord God said, it is not good that man should be alone; I will make him a help meet for him." My thought is if being alone in the Garden of Eden, which was Paradise, was not good enough, imagine staying in this world as we know it. When people make marriage vows, God hands us serious responsibilities. He tasks us with protecting each other from the experience of loneliness.

Being alone is literally the opposite of oneness, and that is not God's intention for marriage. In Genesis 2:24, the Bible says, "Therefore shall a man leave his father and his mother, and shall cleave unto his wife: and they shall become one flesh." Some people mistake "one flesh" for sexual intimacy, but it is way more than that. It has to do with spiritual intimacy, support, friendship, and comfort. Honest communication and open-mindedness are key traits of a successful marriage. All of these blend together to create a strong bond in any relationship. You have to bear in mind that if any of these traits is missing, then oneness is not complete.

Because we are married does not mean we may not feel lonely. Marriage sometimes feels like the loneliest place in the world, especially when each partner is lost in their own world of struggles, sadness, and trials. In the creation story, Eve was made to complete Adam. So when the one partner God has chosen for you to be your companion is not meeting up with your spiritual, physical, social, and emotional needs, you can feel all alone. This can lead to discouragement, resentment, depression, anger, and frustration.

The more intimate we are with our partners, the closer we are to them. It takes some time to know a partner well enough, and it is true that we may never fully understand our partners because of the changes they undergo through their spiritual journeys and life experiences. To develop intimacy for your spouse, you will need to sacrifice your own needs to meet theirs. We experience the purest kind of love when our partners delight in sacrificing everything for us. As a man of God, I have made countless sacrifices for my members, but sometimes I unconsciously expect my family and wife to make such sacrifices for me.

Most people cannot endure the kind of marital hardship I have. But I believed and was convinced that God wanted me to keep all the marital vows I made before Him. I will be discussing some ways I was able to save my marital relationship and keep the vows I made before God. I hope other ministers of God who are having marital issues can learn from this.

I committed to trusting God with all my heart: Before one can find peace and joy in a relationship, the person must make some big decision. Will you love God with all your heart and soul more than you love your flesh? How far are you willing to go to preserve your relationship with your spouse? What is holding you from doing that? The better you understand these questions and ways to answer them, the more you can overcome your fears. If you live according to the will of God, there is no way you will not come out victorious. The Bible says, in I Colossians 3:14, "And above all these, put on love and enfold yourselves with the bond of perfectness which binds everything together completely in harmony." I knew that my trials and tests in marriage were aimed at derailing from the path of righteousness, so I stayed firm. I put all my love to work, and God answered me when it mattered. Also, John 4:34 says, "My food is to do the will of Him who sent me, and to accomplish His works." This is another part of the Bible that advocates for total trust in God and all His plans for us.

I began to know God's character: A writer once wrote, "Everything about our lives is determined and influenced by our view of God. Once you see God as he is, you'll see your life in a whole new light." I can say that I have experienced it all in my life. Some will ask, how did I apply it in my marriage? When you consider God's sovereignty and understand that He is the ruler of the universe, then you will realize that He can control any circumstance in our lives and every person He has given to us as a partner. Even if your partner is not getting it right, trust that God is using it to glorify His name in the end. It may be a test of faith to make sure you become victorious and stronger in the faith. Knowing the character of God will keep you from dealing with fear or anxiety about your current situation or the future. After all, in Psalm 27:13, the Bible says, "I would have despaired unless I had believed that I would see the goodness of the Lord in the land of the living." Know this and be calm.

I committed to studying God's word and obeying it: Disciplining yourself to study the Bible regularly is a good step. The Bible says in Luke 11:28, "Blessed are those who hear the word of God and observe it." It helps you know God in a more intimate way, provide guidance and comfort, and helps you deal with the trials and tribulations of a difficult marriage. God's word is a source of great wisdom, encouragement, comfort, and vision. It gave me great peace while I was dealing with the difficult decisions and situations with my partner.

I prayed and prayed: While I was going through those difficult times, I learned to turn to God in prayer. Prayer is a very powerful tool that will get you to the place you need to be. It can reach the heart of any partner. During those hard times, I was praying for God's direction, and I am sure my wife was praying. I am sure this was the reason everything worked out for me.

I made up my mind to love, whether the love is returned or not: People who saw me in my times of trials and tribulations wondered how I was able to stay happy and joyful through those trying times. One thing was for sure, and I was not joyful at the time. However, I decided to practice the principles of love, no matter the circumstances. I made the conscious decision with God's help.

All I am trying to say is, a marriage is ordained by God to help the life and ministry of ministers and children of God. If a minister loses value for a partner, they lose value for a significant part of their ministry and vice versa.

After more than thirty-four years of marriage, I started to have little doubts about my marriage. This is one of the regrets of my life because I should not have doubted my wife and God-given partner for a second. She was supposed to be my pillar and my strength during those trying times, but I was too blind to see it that way. I was so focused on survival and making it through those times that I forgot about the importance of a partner. She was not only my physical partner, she was my spiritual partner, but I neglected it when the pressure of my trials became too much. But God was going to prove to me that I needed a woman like her in my life. I never doubted and would never doubt the power of God. He used my trials and tribulations to show me a lot of things, one of them was the kind of wife God gave me. Where do I start? First, let me start with the care my wife showered on me while I was going through health challenges. One week before I was admitted to the hospital, my wife laid in my bed. In fact, she was there for a whole week. She did not leave my side, even though I was suffering from COVID-19. We all know it was a contagious virus, but I believe that God kept her safe to care for me. She spent most of her time beside me, yet she did not contract the virus. I got scared for her and even urged her to leave, but she did not want to leave my side.

At that time, I knew I had a partner I did not cherish enough. Going through the risk of contracting a virus as deadly as COVID-19 was the height of love she had for me. I got ill in 2020, no thanks to the COVID-19 pandemic. I have never been one to support going to the hospital, and I always believed that my body was strong enough to withstand any disease or illness that came my way. However, during that time, I believe I felt so ill that I knew it was time to call a doctor. I told my wife to call 911, and you needed to see the surprise on her face. She could not believe that I was actually seeking medical assistance, considering it was against what I have stood for most of my life. Everyone close to me knows I am not a big fan of EMS. At this point, my family, and most especially, my wife, knew I was really sick. My wife became a little afraid, and she began to pray and plead the blood of Jesus over my life and my health. I could see that she was scared, and she was very frantic in her actions. After calling 911, she kept covering me spiritually with the blood of Jesus while we waited for the ambulance. We waited and waited, and all this while, she kept praying and praying. While I laid on the bed, I could literally feel my last breath is drawn. I was too weak to pray physically, but in my mind, I kept asking God to keep me alive. I reminded God of all the plans He has for me, how He wants me to lead His sheep, guide my successor, and prepare me fully for the international ministry. All these kept running through my mind as my body began to deteriorate, and I felt helpless at some point. But God is God, and he always steps in at the right time. In my moments of weakness and spiritual despair, God said something to me, "If you ever doubted for a minute that this is your wife; I have used this moment to prove to you that she is really your wife. I made her specifically for you." When I heard the voice, I looked up and saw my wife, still praying and covering me with the blood of Jesus. I was too weak to smile, but I managed one. I felt blessed to know that my life meant so much to my wife.

During those trying times, I was too blind to understand that she was the one God made for me. I kept seeing my marital problems as a fault on her part, but God had other plans. He meant to show me that she was the one for me. Some may even think He used extreme measures, but the Bible says in Isaiah 55:8-9, "For my thoughts are not your thoughts, neither are your ways my ways, declares the Lord. For as the heavens are higher than the earth, so are my ways higher than your ways, and my thoughts than your thoughts." So how God chose to reveal my gem to me does not matter to me; what matters is the fact that I found it.

In those moments, I was able to realize something. My wife was one of the untapped resources in my life. As a minister of God, I never truly realized that she was supposed to be my source of spiritual upliftment. She performed her duties as a wife and as a mother to my children, but I never really allowed her to show me her full spiritual potential.

When I laid on the sickbed, I could feel the power of God all over me as she was praying. I could feel the heavens moving in her favour. I was too weak to pray, but I knew God was at work, answering the prayers of my wife. She tapped into my anointing and joined her faith with mine. I had never felt so moved by the presence of God in my life than at that point. In fact, I would say my wife was an untapped well. Sometimes, I feel bad, knowing I was not able to tap from her wealth of spiritual resources. It was like I had realized I made a mistake with her as I laid on that bed. All I was asking God was to help me live long enough to tap into the wealth of resources I just discovered. While all these were running through my mind, she kept praying and asking God to heal me. She did not realize what was going on with me.

One day, I was preaching and said, "God will allow us to sit in the dark to learn how to see what we could not see in the light." When it all started to come down on me, I realized that maybe, I might have been talking to myself at that time. I kept wondering as I was in that dark place of my life. When it all felt like the world was falling apart, I asked God, "Father, what is happening? Why is my world crumbling so fast?" All these questions seemed to tamper with my faith, and I was not about to let it. During that time, I was practically at the lowest point of my life. But I am sure that God used that moment to lead me into the light as he always does. So, my question is, if you are going through those tough times, why don't you trust God to help you through those times and make you victorious in the end? As I said before, if I survived last year, I believe nothing is too much for God to do.

I am a living testimony of the trials and tribulations of marriage and other life problems. But by the grace of God, I can confidently tell you that I survived whatever life challenges came my way. I am grateful to Almighty God for making me learn these spiritual principles. Today, my marriage is no longer the struggle it used to be. Our marriage has become more peaceful than ever, and I have been given a second chance to tap from the wealth of spiritual resources my wife has. Now, I see her as a wife, companion, lover, and spiritual support. You can also thrive in difficult marriages, no matter if you are a minister or a child of God. You can experience intimacy with God in ways you never thought existed. Now that my marriage has become a success story, I have asked myself this very important question, what can people see through my spouse that will bring both spiritual and physical healing to their marriages and me?

I want to be a shining light to most people, especially the younger generation. It is always my joy, and I believe it is my purpose to make sure that I pass the right message to the younger generation. I believe marriage plays a big part in the ministry of Christ, and mine was no exception. Even though there were a lot of troubles in my marriage, I was able to conquer by God's grace. I want people, especially the younger generation, to understand that God is there to see them through no matter what the problem is. I know that a lot of marriages have been undergoing a lot of challenges. In fact, when I look at some of the ministers, they seem to be having failed marriages. It does not mean that they do not serve God or are not called by Him; I believe it is because they have not been able to perceive through these hard times. I admit it was so difficult for me to scale through, and I picture what young marriages are going through. As a minister of God, I have been counselling a lot of young couples, and I hear a lot of stories. Most of them seem not to understand that a marriage is not all rosy. They do not want to believe that there may be hard times or those times they would face some challenges as a couple. I always try to encourage them to stay true to each other. Failed marriages are not God's plans for his people. The Bible says, in

Proverbs 18:22, "He who finds a wife finds a good thing, and obtains favor from the Lord." This means that whenever a man finds a wife, they have both found good things. If you are a minister, your spouse should be a good addition. As a child of God, your spouse adds good things to your life. We need to tell ourselves the truth; the ministry of God begins at home. There is a popular saying that goes, "Charity begins at home." This means that, as ministers, we need to start our ministry from our household. The ministry of love and care should first start with showing love and care for our wives and children before extending to the flock we are guiding. How can a minister of God not show care to his family and claim to love and show care to the church? It is not done that way.

I can say that I love my wife now more than ever. I see her as the joy of my life, my peace-giver, and the one who makes me smile. All these attributes are God-given, and I am happy that she is my wife. I can also say that the dark season I experienced was enough for me to realize who I truly married. I kept asking God what was happening to my marriage through those times of heartbreak and dejection. Now, I realize that God was actually saying to me, "I will show you the type of woman your wife is, and you will complain no more after that." It was nice to know that God answered my prayers. Whenever I look at my wife now, she radiates all the energy of a goddess, and I believe she is one. I have found the purpose of my marriage. If anyone asks me, what is the purpose of your marriage? I can confidently answer the person by saying, "The purpose of my marriage is to be with a partner that helps me both spiritually and physically. A partner that helps me serve God better, and a partner I will not trade for anything in the world." God can take care of any situation, no matter how difficult it is. The good thing is, God works at His own pace. He can enter a situation and solve it in a minute or take time to answer prayers. All that happens is always to the glory of God.

The healing process of my marriage took about a week. It was a seven-day process. God took His time to do wonders in my marriage. Who am I to ask why it took so long or so short when I am happy with the outcome? I remain blessed that my family is back again, and my wife and I share a love that is stronger than ever. So for all those who are in struggling marriages, I hope you take a cue from what happened to me right now. I need you to believe the same thing will work for you, claim it, and put in the work. God is never too late, and what He says He will do, He will definitely do it. There is no need to worry yourself about it. Just pray, breathe, do what you can as a human, and let God do the rest for you. That is how it works.

When things go wrong with you, there is one thing you need to do for yourself; guess what it is? Take out the positives in every situation. For a student, when you write an exam and it does not go so well, see it as an opportunity to do better. The same applies to every area in which you face trials and tribulation. In my marital trials and temptations, the bright light I saw was the potential of my wife. A woman I used to neglect not because I want to but because of my struggles at the time turned out to be whom God used to save my marriage. As a wife, she was doing her wifely duties and her spiritual duties. Imagine a woman who stayed beside me through my health struggles, even at the risk of contracting the deadly COVID-19 virus. She persevered and would not leave my side, spending all of her time praying for me to get better and better every minute. I do not think all women have it in them to do it. I also believe that God looked down upon my wife, heard her prayers, healed me, and blessed our marriage once more. I will never get tired of saying that my wife is a well of untapped spiritual resources, and it is up to me to tap into them. I always thank God for giving me that chance to enjoy my wife, and I am doing so with all my heart. I would never let such an opportunity pass me by anymore. My wife is my everything, and I am so proud of her. It is not spiritually healthy to hold onto regrets because I would have asked why I had not seen her long before now? But now that I have seen her, I believe it is best to enjoy every moment with her. Also, as I am about to begin my international ministry, I need her by my side for the tough trials ahead. Leaving my local ministry for my son to carry on was hard enough, but I know deep within my heart that the international ministry will be a lot harder. That is why I need my gem beside me for the journey ahead.

I have to talk about another problem people seem to be having in terms of marital struggles. It is the issue of pride. Sometimes, the man of the house seems to be the problem of the marriage. I am not saying that women are not at fault some of the time, but mostly the man who gets it all wrong. What do I mean? The Bible says, in Galatians 6:3, "For if a man think himself to be something, when he is nothing, he deceiveth himself." What I want you to get from this verse is very easy. A man is actually the head of the family, but he is still under the church. On the other hand, Christ is the head of the church. This simply means that Christ is above any man, no matter how big that man thinks he is.

Another part of the Bible, Proverbs 16:18, says, "Pride goeth before destruction, and a haughty spirit before a fall." So when a man thinks highly of himself, it can be termed "Pride." The general dictionary meaning of pride is, "A sense of one's self-worth, and the abhorrence of what is beneath or unworthy of one." I may not be an English language professor, but I want to get out two points from this definition.

- The first is that pride is a sense of one's self-worth. If I am not mistaken, we all have our self-worth, and it is not reasonable to act below that self-worth. I want to relate it to the spiritual aspect. Do you know that there is a certain level one would get in the spirit, even the devil becomes afraid of them? Without self-worth, some miracles would not happen. The major and minor prophets of the Bible worked with a very high level of self-worth. Elijah, for example, was able to make declarations, knowing that God would honour it no matter what happens. It was the same with the other prophets. Their spiritual self-worth made it possible for them to move the heavens and the earth with spoken words of their mouth. This is the first part.

- The second part I want to get out from the same verse is, "THE ABHORRENCE OF WHAT IS BENEATH OR UNWORTHY OF ONE." This should be the part with greater emphasis. I believe this is where most men get it wrong. The Lord has made you the head of your home, but you should understand that it is not possible to do it all alone. If it was possible, God would not have made Adam a helper to help him. He is God, and He sees the end from the beginning. If He created a helper for man, it means that man really needs a helper. Man, in this case, a husband, should not do himself a disservice by thinking that it is possible to do everything alone. It is not possible. You will need the support of your spouse, and that is what marriage should be all about—standing in and supporting each other. I know that pride is one of the reasons for many failed marriages in the world today, and even among the ministers of God. When a man is wrong, he ought to admit that he is wrong. It does not change his status as the head of the family, and the earlier Christians and ministers understand that the better things will go in most marriages in the world. I also want to point out that the word "Man", when used in the Bible, applies to man and woman alike. The Bible mostly refers to everyone with the term "Man", so nobody is exempted from the rules and instruction of the Bible. The point is, even a woman needs her man to be spiritually productive, just as the man needs his woman. Everybody has their role to play in the ministry of God, and it is important that we do our part diligently. The Lord wishes it to be so.

The sweetest and encouraging part of going through marital struggles is looking up during those difficult times and seeing that your partner is fully by your side. It comes with a certain level of comfort and joy. As I said, what pulled me through those hard times was the fact that I had a loving wife. Up until that time, I never knew how important my wife was. This part of the Bible, "He who finds a wife finds a good thing, and obtains favor from the Lord", kept playing in my head all the time. I began to understand what the Lord meant by that bible verse. It went to show that God already destined every wife as a source of strength, support, and inspiration to her husband. After my marital struggles, I finally confirmed something, "Whenever you go through a difficult stage of your life, and your spouse is there for you, know that you have true love." Not every marriage can boast of true love. I have seen many marriages that ended because there is no true love. As a marriage counsellor, I have always understood that lack of true love is what ends marriages prematurely. I always thought marriage was rosy and smooth until I met my challenges. I started to understand what some of these couples were going through. I am not saying it is an excuse to end marriages prematurely. God will always see you through, just as He saw me through. I learned many things from all the failed marriages I encountered, and I learnt even more from mine. Now, I believe I have become a better counsellor, considering all the experiences I have gathered from other experiences and mine. All I am saying is, it is understandable to have marital problems but unacceptable to end marriages because of them.

7

God Healed It All

"So do not fear, for I am with you; do not be dismayed, for I am your God. I will strengthen you and help you; I will uphold you with my righteous right hand." - Isaiah 41:10.

Let us talk more about healing. I can say that God healed all my wounds, marital, spiritual, and physical. But there are some things I learned about healing, and I want to share them with you. I will be focusing my attention on what the Bible says about healing and how Christians can pray to be healed. Spiritual healing is very much different from physical healing, so Christians must visit the Bible for guidance and direction. The biblical way is the best way to approach the aspect of spiritual healing, and in the scripture, we can always discover the purpose and source of healing, as well as how to ask in Faith. There are some things the Bible says about healing and prayer. In no particular order, they are:

- **Both spiritual and spiritual healing only comes from God:** I do not want to condemn the importance of doctors and medical practitioners, but they may be caretakers, but God is the healer. Only God has the power to heal someone totally. In Psalm 103:2-3, the Bible says, "Bless the Lord, O my soul, and forget not all His benefits. Who forgiveth all thine iniquities; who healeth all thy diseases?" This verse goes to show that God can heal anyone completely. Isaiah 38:15-16 talks about physical healing. Psalm 34:18 stresses that God can also heal spiritually, and Daniel 4:34 discusses God's mental healing power. In general, we, as Christians, have to understand that the Holy Spirit, in accordance with the spiritual gifts of the believer, can heal every wound.

- **Healing is biblical**: One of the gifts of the Holy Spirit to the church is healing, as evident in I Corinthians 14:1. He distributes healing according to His will. Healing is common for the growth of the church, and it comes to us in glorification and honour of God's name. While Jesus was on earth, He spread the gospel through healing and advocated His disciples to do the same with His power and authority.

- **We, as Christians, may be the problem:** Using the Bible as our book of the law, we will understand that there are some things we do or don't do that tampers with our healing. For example, in James 5:16, the Bible says, "Confess your sins to each other, and pray for each other so that you may be healed...." This is trying to tell us that there are some things we need to do for healing to occur. Also, we need to understand that it is not every time that we are responsible for the afflictions and tests that come our way. Jesus said, in John 9:1-13, that the blind man was not guilty of any sin that may have caused his blindness, and neither were his parents.

Also, a lack of Faith or not surrendering to God's purposes may also be reasons some Christians hinder their healing. Look at Romans 8:28-29. Believers need to believe and understand that everything is interwoven into God's perfect plan. In James 5:15, the Bible says, "And the prayer of faith shall save the sick, and the Lord shall raise him up; and if he have committed sins, they shall be forgiven." However, we must remember that faith without work is useless. You cannot say you have Faith when you are not working according to the plan and purpose of God.

- **We, as Christians, should know that we should not fail to open our mouths and ask for healing:** In John 5:6-7, the Bible says, "When Jesus saw him lie, and knew that he had been now a long time in that case, he saith unto him, wilt thou be made whole?" That was not an irrelevant question. It simply means that God wants us to ask before He does His wonders. In Matthews 7:7, the Bible says, "Ask and it shall be given you; seek, and ye shall find; knock and it shall be opened unto you;" This highlights the importance of asking for a miracle.

- **God decides when to heal and when not to:** Looking at Numbers 12:1-15, we would understand that God chooses when to heal and when not to. He did not heal Miriam's leprosy immediately. Another example in the Bible was when God refused to heal Ahaziah because of his pagan ways in 2 Kings 1:1-17. There are other instances in the Bible where the Lord refused to heal someone immediately, doing it at his own time. The God that sent his only son to die for our sins is a loving Father. So whenever He does not heal someone, it may be to sanctify the person through afflictions and trials.

- **Question yourself thoroughly as a believer:** There is a very clear difference between questioning your stand with God and self-doubt. With self-doubt, there may be no healing because your Faith may be shaken. But questioning yourself will put you on the right track to righteousness. Most people believe that going to church makes them true believers. I am writing to say that is not true. In Psalm 139:1-2, the

Bible lets us understand that God knows everything that goes on in our hearts. It says, "O Lord, thou hast searched me, and known me. Thou knowest my downsitting and mine uprising, thou understandest my thought afar off." So you cannot deceive God. When you pray for healing, ask yourself these questions:

a. Do I live a life that pleases God?

b. Do I have the required amount of Faith and courage to ask God for healing?

c. Is there any doubt in my mind that healing will come?

- **Christians need to understand that both healing and afflictions serve their different purposes:** In Isaiah 55:8-9, it is clear that our thoughts are so different from God's thoughts. Sometimes, God brings healing just to glorify his name. This is demonstrated in the book of

John 11:1-45. Other times, God withholds healing for different purposes. Whatever is your Faith, you just need to accept it, pray for grace, and understand that God's plans for us are always thoughts of good.

- **Finally, no matter what we go through, we will be ultimately healed in heaven:** Most Christians do not want to hear this, but for a true believer who died in Christ Jesus, ultimate healing comes through death. Scary as it may sound, it is evident in Revelation 21:4, "And God shall wipe away all tears from their eyes; and there shall be no more death, neither sorrow, nor crying, neither shall there be any more pain; for the former things are passed away." Nobody wants to be sick, both in mind and body, and definitely, nobody wants to die, but if you are in Christ Jesus, all is well.

Now, what are those steps we can take to be completely healed? Remember that even in a real-life scenario, after surviving some tragic event, you will need some time and take some steps to heal. It is just the same way in the spiritual aspect. The Great Physician, God Almighty, is able to heal all wounds completely and mend the broken heart. Just like doctors give instructions on what to do and what not to do during healing, we have our own parts to play to heal spiritually. God also wants us to work with Him in the healing process. Spiritual healing may be sudden and immediate, or it can be a process. Nobody said it was going to be easy though, all I am saying is these steps need to be taken to heal spiritual wounds completely. The healing may take longer than we want but be rest assured that God can heal us once and for all. So, what are these steps?

- **Clean the wound:** Just like physical wounds, spiritual wounds should be cleaned thoroughly to prepare for complete healing. This can be a very painful process, and I must acknowledge it. Spiritually, we can clean our wounds with prayers and fasting. I remember praying and fasting when I was going through my trials and temptations. Knowing that God was listening gave me all the encouragement I needed. We must go to God in fasting and prayer, asking Him to do what He does best; heal. We must also be willing to receive our healing without a doubt. During prayer, we must ask God to forgive us for all our mistakes. In 1 John 1:9, the Bible says, "If we confess our sins, He is faithful and just to forgive us our sins, and cleanse us from all unrighteousness." During trials and temptations, we make a lot of mistakes. I can tell you this because I made mine, and one of the biggest mistakes I made was not recognizing the wealth of spiritual resources my wife possessed. We should also ask Him to give us the grace to forgive ourselves and others. Bitterness, resentfulness, strife, hurt, anger, self-pity, guilt, etc., are those toxins that need to be cleaned out of our spiritual wounds. The thorough cleansing prepares us for the healing process proper, and forgiveness is the greatest tool for this cleansing.

- **Guard the wound against infections:** Just like physical wounds can be protected from harmful substances and toxins, we can always guard our spiritual wounds against things that can hinder the healing process or even cause more harm than good. In Psalm 147:3, the Bible says, "He heals the brokenhearted and binds up their wounds." This shows clearly that God is working to heal us, but we must do our own part. Someone might ask, what exactly can I do to guard the wound?

We can do that by renewing our minds. The mind is a powerful weapon that helps to heal spiritual wounds. We can see that in Romans 12:2, where the Bible says, "And do not be conformed to this world, but be transformed by the renewing of your mind that you may prove what is that good, acceptable and perfect will of God." We need to guard our minds against those spiritual toxins that we have already cleansed from the wound and focus on the good plans God has for us while He works on our healing.

- **Keep monitoring the wound:** Like physical wounds, when spiritual wounds are not closely monitored, there is a high risk of infection. 1 Peter 5:8 says, "Be sober, be vigilant; because your adversary the devil walks about like a roaring lion, seeking whom he may devour." When a spiritual wound is infected, it spreads quickly to other parts of our lives, affecting our relationship with God and man and even our Faith. If this happens, we may be worse off from where we started the healing process. So we must guard against any toxins so we can be completely healed. We must continue to clean, guard, and monitor our wounds until they heal and maybe leave us with scars that may act as reminders of what God has done for us.

In the end, I can say that in the end, God healed my finances, my ministry, and everything concerning me during those dark times in 2020. I have been retired for a while now. Before then, I used to work, but one day, I heard the voice of God say, "Leave your job, and serve me in the ministry full-time." I knew it was the voice of God from the beginning, and I wasted no time quitting my job and signing up for God to use me to do His work. However, during the pandemic, I rushed back to my work in a bid to make ends meet. Something strange happened. My business began to have issues, and it started dwindling. At that moment, I had to remember what God said to me. He said, "I will take care of your finances as long as you go into full-time ministry."

I was guilty of trying to help God do His work, and He punished me by dwindling my finances. It was a wake-up call, and I had to answer. I realized at that moment that just because situations change does not mean that the word of God will change. In Malachi 3:7, the Bible says, "For I am the Lord, I change not; therefore ye sons of Jacob are not consumed." Two things can be learned from this bible verse. One, God confirmed it once again that He changeth not, so no matter what it is you are going through, you can be sure that God changeth not. I tried to change my own plans because of the pandemic and economic crisis I was going through. I almost lost sight of the fact that I was dealing with the Almighty God who permitted the coronavirus pandemic and economic crisis to happen so that his name can be glorified. Second, God will never let you be consumed. Even during those times, God showed Himself to be God. He created me, so how did I even think for a second that I was going to help God? I say it again; He showed Himself to be God.

After COVID, God caused my needs to change. One minute, I was struggling with my health, the next minute, God changed my need to that of repentance. The surprising thing is, God made me realize that those things I thought were my immediate needs were actually not my needs at all. Instead, my eyes and mentality were refocused. During my trying times, my immediate needs were how to save my marriage, make some money, and save my ministry. The needs did not change totally; only God's forgiveness took precedence over those other needs. When God forgave me, every other thing fell into place, and I became whole again. I keep thanking God for everything.

What exactly was I apologetic and seeking repentance for? I may have said this a million times, but the truth is I was asking God to forgive me. I had to specially ask God to forgive me for doubting Him. I tried to do it on my own, and I failed to realize that God is the author and finisher of our Faith.

All I needed was God's forgiveness, and every other thing began to fail in place. First, I began to see changes in my marital relationship. My wife and I began to blossom like a young couple who just got married. It was like my wife was young again, but I knew it was the radiation of her happiness that made her look beautiful. My family began to share happy moments, and even my children were not left out.

Next, I began to see the finger of the Lord in my finances. I did not have to go back to any work for doors to begin to open financially. I began to enjoy blessings from every point of my life. Favour kept pursuing my family and me, and the lack we experienced was gone for good. Whenever a financial favour came, I knelt down, looked up to God and smiled, saying, "Lord, I know it was you." I was never wrong because I knew it was God that kept making things happen in my life.

Just like Job in the Bible, God restored me a hundred folds. Everything came back to life, and even better. I have never felt happier in my life. Just knowing that God was there for me all through those times kept urging me to do more, and I want to do more for the glory of God. The overflow was already there the whole time. I just did not realize it on time. It was just the case of a dam that held water for so long. My blessing was held by my heart. All the transgressions I committed during my trying times acted as the dam that held my blessings. The moment God forgave me, the walls of the dam exploded, and my household could not contain it.

During those times, I was struggling; I had some people I could run to in those times of despair. I have said that no man is an island, and God would not come from heaven to help His children. He would use other people to reach out to us. My spiritual helpers helped me in different ways. With the counselling, prayers, fasting, and encouragement, everything went according to God's plan. However, there was something I learnt during those times. God used the hard times to remove some people from my life. In the spiritual race to make heaven, some people may be considered dead weight. By dead weight, I mean those things that pull you back and do not allow you to reach your full potential. Whoever left our lives when we were going through hard times was never really meant to be there in the first place. This boils down to God's ultimate plan to perfect our lives. I actually thought I lost a lot of friends and family during those times, but knowing what I know now, I can say that I did not lose anything. All God did was remove the chaff from the grain and make me a better minister. Let me dwell on this a bit. In my experience, there are five major reasons God can remove people from our lives. It happened in mine, so I thought I would share the experience with you. First and foremost, we need to understand that people come into our lives and go. Those you may have expected to stick around may have gone out of your life for different reasons. In my case, most of them left because of my trials and tribulations. I am glad that some stayed, and I cherish them because now I realize that they are the ones for me. We serve God with the master plan. Things do not just happen randomly when God is in control. In Ecclesiastes 3:1, the Bible says, "To everything, there is a season, and a time to every purpose under the heaven." This means that we can always trust God's plans for us. I must state again; God allows some things to happen in our life, just so that His name will be glorified. Tests and trials build our Faith and character. There is a popular saying, "There is no victory in comfort", and if bad things happened to Jesus Christ, surely it can happen to us. In the same vein, since Jesus was able to rise above all the trials and tribulations, so can we. So why do people disappear from our lives?

- **To fulfill the plan and purpose of God:** If you are a true believer, you need to trust that God will take care of us. That trust comes with giving Him the wheel of our lives for Him to lead us wherever he sees fit. Therefore, when God is in control, he regulates whoever comes and leaves our lives. In Jeremiah 29:11, the Bible says, "For I know the thoughts that I think toward you, saith the Lord, thoughts of peace, and not of evil, to give you an expected end." So when His plans involve removing people from your life, you should be happy and grateful.

- **That person may be needed somewhere else:** We need to come to terms with the fact that God can remove someone from our lives for something positive. It just might be that God wants to use that person to bless someone else. It may be a bit complicated for a human mind to understand, especially if the person was so close to you. You should bear in mind that God also has a plan for that person, just as He has for you. So that person may just be needed to serve God's purpose somewhere else. In Exodus 4:18, Moses begged Jethro, his father-in-law, to let him go and minister to his brothers. He had a very close relationship with Jethro, but he was needed somewhere else, so he had to go. It could still happen in our lives too.

- **That person may not be the right person for you:** This is the most popular reason among Christians. Once someone leaves our lives, we are often too quick to jump to this conclusion. Fortunately, it could be correct. When someone leaves your life, God may be trying to tell you that the person is not right for you. As a mysterious God, you might just be reunited with the person in the near future or not; you never can tell. Romans 8:28 tells us that "all things work together for good to them that love God, to them who are the called according to his purpose."

- **They may be toxic to your Faith:** You may encounter a lot of people in your life every day without knowing who is toxic or not. Some may secretly hate you, and you will unsuspectedly see them as your friends. They may be able to fool you, but God? No way. How is it even possible to fool your creator? He sees the secret thoughts of everyone and hears every conversation held in secret. In 1 Samuel 16:7, the Bible says, "...for the Lord seeth not as man seeth: for man looketh on the outward appearance, but the Lord looketh on the heart." Since He is our creator, He knows our threshold, and if someone threatens our peace or relationship with him, we need to remove that person from our life.

- **That person may have left your life because God has prepared something better:** Sometimes, we hold onto things and people, thinking that our world revolves around them. God always has something better for us, and that is why He is a great architect. You may be looking at things as losses, but how can it be a loss when God did not ordain it to be there? God is always waiting for us to trust Him wholeheartedly, and He is ready to open His floodgates for the blessings to fall. In fact, 1 Corinthians 2:9 says, "But as it is written, Eye hath not seen, nor ear heard, neither have entered into the heart of man, the things which God hath prepared for them that love Him." The earlier we understand that God is our master planner, the better. Even if we go astray, He is always trying to bring us back. Come to think of it, if we all go astray and He does not bring us back, who is going to enjoy all those good plans He has for us?

Knowing everything happens for a reason, it is always easier to learn from every experience. For instance, if someone left your life because of what you did wrong, now you can always learn to do better. And when God removes anyone from our lives, we should not hold on too long. If you did nothing wrong, then that is God's finger at work. No human being knows the future, but at least we know who holds the future. When I was done, that was when God began to raise people to help me and my ministry. I was so awed by the power of God that I began to give Him thanks and glory for everything He was doing. People I never thought existed were the same people God used to change my story and my ministry. I was getting ministered to from every area of my life. Ministers came flocking into my life, rendering all the help and support I needed. It was great. I can confidently say that what I experienced changed the impact and scope of my ministry.

Young people in my ministry have an urge to rise up and lead. In Ecclesiastes 12:1, the Bible says, "Remember now thy Creator in the days of thy youth, while the evil days come not, nor the years draw nigh, when thou shalt say, I have no pleasure in them." I am very happy when I see young people develop that hunger to serve God. There are a lot of benefits youths can derive from serving the Lord in their youth. I want to discuss with you some of the benefits of serving God in your youth. I have seen these things in the youth of my church, and I believe it is part of my ministry to reach out to the youth as well. The benefits are:

- **Accountability and responsibility:** When young people serve in the house of the Lord, they learn how to be more responsible. Learning responsibility comes in a variety of ways. Whether they are ushers who show people to their seats or hold the door open for visitors, they are all different ways they learn responsibility. They also learn to be accountable whenever they are put in charge of different positions. They start to see themselves as leaders at a very early stage of their lives, and I was impressed when I saw these traits in the youth of my church.

- **Confidence boosting:** When a youth takes up the mantle to serve and lead, their overall confidence levels are boosted. By the time they have handled a couple of positions as young leaders, there is no limit to where their ministry will reach. However, a little encouragement and belief from the older generation will also go a long way to help boost their confidence.

- **It helps build healthy relationships with God and his people:** As young leaders in the church who have the urge to serve God and His people, the only way they can do that is by building a healthy relationship with the God they choose to serve and His people. It even helps them in real-life situations because they become better at relating with other people, even outside the church.

- **When the hunger is there to serve God in your youth, you find spiritual mentors:** I can say that my dad was my spiritual mentor. In the same way, I am the spiritual mentor of my son. This simply means that when you have the urge and hunger to serve God, there has to be that spiritual father or mentor who may have been in your position a long time ago and is willing to help you on your path to righteousness. There is no better place to find spiritual mentors than in the house of the Lord. My ministry is blessed with a lot of God-fearing men and women who are ready to help the hungry youth to serve God. I always feel blessed for that.

- **It helps them realize their gifts and talents early enough:** Just like Jesus had disciples, a minister of God should also have youths to take on the mantle after they are gone. By catching them young, you will observe that there are a lot of talents and gifts

God has embedded in a lot of youths, but because they have not gotten a chance to display those God-given talents, some of them go to waste. If a youth is willing to serve God and lead his people, what better place than the house of God to show it? Every talent God gives the youth is to serve Him.

- **They are encouraged to go into full-time ministry:** When the youth start having the hunger to lead and serve God, they need to be encouraged to continue in the ministry. With time, they are given bigger responsibilities, and in the near future, they will be ready to take on the mantle of leadership and carry on the ministry. That was the exact case with my son. With the hunger and zeal I saw in him, I encouraged him to serve God, and now, he is prepared to take the mantle of local ministry from me. When youths have an urge to lead, they learn to put others before themselves: The youth who have a hunger to lead and serve to end up learning to put others before themselves. The Bible says that for one to lead, one must first become a servant. Jesus was a perfect example of a leader who served His people with His ministry.

- **With a hunger to lead and serve, the youth become examples for the even younger generation:** Youths who are exposed to Christ turn out to be shining lights for the younger generation. The more exposed they are to Christ, the more they learn to emulate his ways. As we said earlier, the younger generation, in this case, the youth, look up to us for direction and guidance. When they exhibit that hunger and zeal to serve the Lord, the younger generation also learns a thing or two from them.

- **When the hunger is there to serve God in your youth, you find spiritual mentors:** I can say that my dad was my spiritual mentor. In the same way, I am the spiritual mentor of my son. This simply means that when you have the urge and hunger to serve God, there has to be that spiritual father or mentor who may have been in your position a long time ago and is willing to help you on your path to righteousness. There is no better place to find spiritual mentors than in the house of the Lord. My ministry is blessed with a lot of God-fearing men and women who are ready to help the hungry youth to serve God. I always feel blessed for that.

- **Serving God in your youth helps you learn more from the Bible:** When the youth become zealous about the things of God, they take up spiritual positions in the church. With great power comes great responsibility, or so they say. So taking up these responsibilities will help them study the Bible more and more. This helps build their spiritual lives and is maybe, one of the most important benefits of serving God in your youth.

In my ministry, there are not a thousand or a million youths. However, there are a few youths with the zeal, drive, and hunger of a thousand, and that is enough for me. Have you ever wondered why God chooses not to work through crowds? Because one person is enough to do God's work. Literally, God is not using one person. The point is, He can use few people to achieve a lot of things. The power of God is not in the numbers; the power of God works through the commitment of the numbers. God can use one soul to convert an entire nation to Himself. He does not need a thousand people to glorify His name. He sent only Jonah to the land of Nineveh, and in the biggest case of all, He sent only Jesus to save the whole world. It would not have been a great deal to send down a host of angels, but the crowd is not necessary to do God's work. I realized that during my times of trials and temptation.

8

My Challenge to God's People

Now is the time to challenge God's people. I have earned the right to challenge God's people, and I am doing that right now. You need to know that I have become an example or point of reference due to my experiences and stories. I went through a lot in 2020. Things went from bad to worse for me in an instant. I never thought I would survive what I did. My marriage was in shambles, my health was not so great, and it felt like I was losing sight of the promise and ministry of God. It is a rough patch that I believe a lot of us have to go through at different points in our life. But one thing is certain; God will not allow a problem that will overwhelm you to come your way. He is our creator, and He created us with all our strengths and weaknesses. Look at it this way,

177

can an earthly father give his five-year-old a bag of flour to carry? No, because He knows that it will overwhelm the child, and He would not want any harm to come to His child. How much more our heavenly Father? Every iota of love we show to our offspring is just trivial when compared to the love that God has for us. He is our Father, and He wants us to be strong in the faith, but He works according to our thresholds, even though we may not understand His ways. Trials and tribulations? I can confidently tell you they are part of God's plans.

My direct challenge to God's people now is, "Do not remove your tools because it gets uncomfortable to wear them." But what do I mean by that? I mean, "Do not give up on God when things become too much." No matter how steadfast we are in prayer, there are times we may feel like God is taking a very long time to answer us and do something to change our situation. In those moments, we begin to doubt the faithfulness of God. At that moment, we begin to "remove our tools because it gets uncomfortable to wear them." As a soldier of God, is it wise to remove your armour of faith just because it has become too heavy due to the number of trials and tribulations we face? Just like in a real-life situation, a warrior cannot go to battle without wearing his armour and carrying his shield. It turns out to be the difference between life and death sometimes. Just in the same way, dropping your spiritual tools because they become too heavy may be the difference between our spiritual life and death. We may lose sight of God's plans when we drop our tools during the storm. I can relate to what I am saying right now. Like I said, during my trials and temptations, I know that deep within my heart, I dropped my tools for a minute. I began to lose the battle in my marriage, finance, and even in my ministry. It was like a flood was carrying me further and further away from God. Like Peter, I was almost overwhelmed by what I saw around me, and I took my eyes off the prize. It seemed that God had forsaken me, just like Jesus said when God turned His eyes away from him on the cross. I cried and cried, begging God to intervene in my life. It was a very rough patch in my life, and I still have the scars to prove it. However, God reminded me with some verses of the bible that He has not forsaken or forgotten me, and I know He never does that to His children. I want to share those verses with you:

"Be joyful in hope, patient in affliction, faithful in prayer"

— Romans 12:12

Being joyful in hope when trials and temptations are all around you can be very difficult. In my case, I can say that I was far from joyful. Knowing my family, business, and health were in shambles threatened to steal my joy away. But in this verse, God instructed me to be patient and pray consistently. God is always working out a great plan for you, even if you do not see it yet.

"Let us not become weary in doing good, for at the proper time, we will reap a harvest if we do not give up"

- Galatians 6:9

Doing the right thing consistently without getting any reward or instant benefit can be really frustrating if you ask me. Yes, it can. It can be difficult, but so is serving God if one does not have faith. Instead of letting go of your fighting tools during hard times, is it not better to keep working in faith and waiting for God's appointed time? In this verse, it is clear that those who persevere will receive a return on their investment. Our actions, words, and faith can make lasting impressions on everyone around us. As I said earlier, the younger generation is working. We never know the legacy we leave behind with our actions. All we have to do is trust that God will bless the works of our hands and give us the grace to be good examples.

"In my distress, I called to the Lord; I called out to my God. From His temple, he heard my voice; my cry came to His ears"

- 2 Samuel 22:7

Whenever we call upon the name of the Lord, He always hears us. That does not mean He will always answer us, but we need to have that conviction that He always does what is best for us. Trusting God even when we do not understand gives us the chance to see what plans He has in our lives. When we seek God's face and genuinely ask for His help, He will open our eyes just like He opened the eyes of Elisha's servant and show us ways to become closer to Him.

"Blessed is the one who perseveres under trial because, having stood the test, that person will receive the crown of life that the Lord has promised to those who love him"

- James 1:12

In those times, we feel like letting our guard down and dropping our spiritual tools of warfare. We need to remember that God has promised us the crown of life. Our reward in our heavenly home is far more precious and is absolutely worth every trial and test we face on earth. In those times of trials and tribulations, I used this trick; I saw myself as a marathon runner. Whenever I felt like giving up, I encouraged myself by saying I am running the last lap. That was how I kept running the last lap till...... God came to my rescue. He saw that I had been exhausted and had reached my threshold, and He stepped in.

God's timing is essential.

"The Lord does not delay and is not tardy or slow about what He promises, according to some people's conception of slowness, but He is long-suffering toward you, not desiring that any should perish, but that all should turn to repentance"
- 2 Peter 3:9

I also want to challenge you to wait for God's time. Let's talk about timing a bit. Without waiting for God's time, survival will mean little or nothing. Have you ever been through trials and temptations? In life, timing is almost everything, both spiritually and physically. Without the right timing, we are prone to lose opportunities to succeed and other possibilities. Timing is critical, and I have to tell you this; you might seem to you like a good idea, but without God's timing, it will not be as fruitful as you want it to be.

Here are some facts you need to know about God's timing. In no particular order, they are:

- **The Holy Spirit is in charge of timing:** Have you ever thought of when the right time is to make a move? Knowing when to do things will increase the chances of success and survival. In Acts 1:7, the bible says, "And he said unto them, it is not for you to know the times or the seasons, which the Father hath put in his own power." From this verse, we must understand one thing, the key to making the right decisions at the best time is the work of the Holy Spirit.

- **You need to be in the right place at the right time:** Sometimes, we may be in the wrong place at the right time or vice versa. That will be a problem, and this is another reason we need the Holy Spirit to lead us aright. In 2 Samuel 11, David was recorded as being at the wrong place at the right time. He was positioned where he was tempted to commit sin after sin and almost lost favour in the eyes of the Lord. He was supposed to be at war with his troops; instead, he stayed back in Jerusalem. So when we are in the wrong place at the right time, there is a high chance we may get things wrong. So while praying for the right time, we need to pray for the Holy Spirit to also put us in the right place at the right time.

- **Delay is never denial:** We may have talked about this earlier, but let me stress the point again. In Habakkuk 2:3, the bible says, "For the vision is yet for an appointed time, and it hastens to the end; it will not deceive or disappoint, though it may tarry, wait earnestly for it, because it will surely come; it will not be behindhand on its appointed day." The longer the time, we may begin to doubt God or question our faith. But we just need to know that God's plan is never a delay.

- **Our time lies in the hands of God:** The Psalmist says, in Psalm 31:15, "My times are in your hands, deliver me from the hands of my foes, and those who pursue me and persecute me." So whenever God delivers you from your trials and tribulations, it is for a purpose.

- **There is always a time for deliverance:** God does not allow His children to suffer trials and tribulations forever. At some point, He is bound by His word to intervene in those trials and tribulations. In 2 Corinthians 6:2, the bible says, "For He says, in the time of favor of an assured welcome, I have listened to and heeded your call, and I have helped you on the day of deliverance. Behold, now is truly the time for a gracious welcome, and acceptance; behold, now is the day of salvation." From this verse, we should understand that God already has plans to deliver us.

He has built us to survive those times; all we have to do is persevere till His appointed time.

I want to tell you something. There is no need to misinterpret discomfort as a failure on your part or punishment from God. As we have said, trials and tribulations are meant to strengthen our faith and make us better Christians. Precious stones in their natural state are so dull and unattractive, but after refining, they are so beautiful. We are the raw metals in their natural ores, and the refining process is what we refer to as our trials and tribulations. That was how I kept seeing myself, as a precious metal that needed refining and glory be to God, I have been thoroughly refined. I look at my life, at the trials and tribulations, at my experiences, and I go down on my knees with one sentence on my lips, "Thank you, Lord." Some people do not understand when I try to explain what I have been through. Luckily for me, I never misinterpreted my discomfort for punishment from God. I am also challenging you to NOT do the same. We may be going through a lot at the moment, but a success story, I speak to that storm in your life, BE CALM! Is it any health problem? The bible says, in Isaiah 53:5, "But he was wounded for our transgressions, he was bruised for our iniquities: the chastisement of our peace was upon him; and with his stripes we are healed." Is it a marital problem? God says in 1 Peter 3:7, "Likewise, husbands, live with your wives in an understanding way, showing honor to the woman as the weaker vessel, since they are heirs with you of the grace of life, so that your prayers may not be hindered." It is also directed to wives in the same chapter. In the first verse of the same chapter, it says, "Likewise, wives, be subject to your own husbands, so that even if some do not obey the word, they may be won without a word by the conduct of their wives." Is it a problem with the ministry of God? Ephesians 3:17-19 tells us, "so that Christ may dwell in your hearts through faith; and that you, being rooted and grounded in love, may be able to comprehend with all the saints what is the breadth and length and height and depth, and to know the love of Christ which surpasses knowledge, that you may be filled up to all the fullness of God." No matter the kind of challenge, trial, or tribulation one is going through, there are verses in the bible to help you get inspired, pick up any useful spiritual tool you may have dropped, and survive just like God wants you to. You just have to dig deep within yourself and find out God's plan for you.

How do we survive through hard times???

1 Corinthians 10:13 reads, "no temptation has overtaken you except such as is common to man." This shows that no trial, test, or challenge is happening for the first time. The general challenges familiar to man are health problems, loss of loved ones, financial and job troubles, emotional problems and troubled relationships, and spiritual problems.

There may be other rare trials and temptations, however, but none is entirely new to man. To survive, Peter instructs us in 1 Peter 5:7, "Cast all your care upon God, for He cares for you." We must always run to God for survival, and that is why He is our Father.

We have been talking about trials and tribulations since the beginning. Now, we are so close to the end. The ultimate question is, how do we survive through hard times? We have talked about it in different sections of this book, but a nice summary would help you get the point a lot easier. Below, I will be summarizing all we have been talking about into seven different points. These are the ways I was able to survive.

I must point out that we are all humans, and with the right amount of pressure from trials and tribulations, we might make a few mistakes. We must remember first to:

Pray for forgiveness: Forgiveness is a big hindrance to God's blessings. Proverbs 28:13 tells us that "You will never succeed in life if you try to hide your sins. Confess them, and give them up; then God will show mercy to you." This means that without forgiveness from God, our trials and tribulations may last a little longer. But once we have asked God to forgive us, we need to.

Pray for faith: When life is very uncertain and the future looks challenging, what do we need to pull us through as children of God? Faith. The bible recorded many places where Jesus used the phrase, "O you of little faith." Surely, that wasn't a coincidence. During times of trials, I had a very simple prayer point, "Lord, please strengthen my faith." 2 Corinthians 5:7 tells us that we should work by faith and not by sight. Sight tells us that God has intervened, but Faith tells us that God will intervene. There is a huge difference. And since things may not come as quick as we want them to, we need to.

Pray for endurance: Sometimes, there may be nothing left in the tank, but we need to stand our ground and withstand the storm. Ephesians 6:13 says, "take up the whole armor of God, that you may be able to withstand in the evil day, and having done all, to stand." I kept hanging on a little longer and longer till God rescued me. We cannot be idle while enduring, so we also need to.

Pray for wisdom and vision: According to James 1:5, the bible says, "If any of you lacks wisdom, let him ask of God, who gives to all liberally and without reproach, ad it will be given to him." Big problems require big decisions. Proverbs 29:18 says, "Where there is no vision, the people perish: but he that kept the law, happy is he." Wisdom and vision are subjects that are too large to explain, but the idea is we need vision and wisdom to survive. When God shows us wisdom, what does it take to do God's will? This is why we need to.

Pray for courage: Joshua 1:5 says, "No man shall be able to stand before you all the days of your life; as I will be with you. I will not leave you nor forsake you." We need to be courageous in times of trials and tribulations, especially in times of failure and suffering. Also, in 1 Corinthians 16:13, the bible says, "Watch, stand fast in the faith, be brave, be strong." Even when we are doing God's will, how do we know and learn to wait for God's time? We can only do this when we.

Pray for patience: James 5:7-8 tells us, "Therefore be patient, brethren, until the coming of the Lord. See how the farmer waits for the precious fruit of the earth, waiting patiently for it until it receives the early and latter rain. You also be patient. Establish your hearts, for the coming of the Lord is at hand." It is funny sometimes when we claim to leave God in control of our life but get impatient with His plans. Being impatient makes you stop living by faith but by the clock. James 1:2-4 says, "My brethren, count it all joy when you fall into various trials, knowing that the testing of your faith produces patience. But let patience have its perfect work, that you may be perfect and complete, lacking nothing." How can one be patient when there is no hope? I hope you now see a reason to.

Pray for hope: Home is seeing beyond the present. It involves seeing what the future holds. Hopelessness may be the most dangerous state of any Christian. Romans 15:13 reads, "the God of hope fill you with all joy and peace in believing, that you may abound in hope by the power of the Holy Spirit." This verse is stressing the fact that as Christians, we need hope to survive.

Pray for your specific needs: Whatever it is we are going through, we need to be specific in our prayers. God knows our thoughts and prayers even before we say them; however, He wants us to say them in supplication and prayer to Him. God, being the Alpha and d Omega, will work according to His plans and purpose in our lives. If He decides to make us wait, best believe it will all be worth it in the end.

I have tried these, and you can see how I turned out fine. I turned out fine does not mean it was easy. I must admit that I struggled with a lot of things. See me as a living testimony. It is my prayer and hopes that whatever it is you are going through, my story would be able to inspire you to survive!

The summary of what we have discussed in this book includes; what survival is, how not to misinterpret our situation or season. We also talked about what a test is. We also dug into the concept of survival, discussing what tools we need for survival. Did we forget that obedience and submission are important for survival? How do we survive without spiritual vision?

Movement coordination is also vital for the survival of a Christian. When we move, we unpack and unload. Once we are done unpacking and unloading, the healing begins. God always finishes any process He starts, so He will definitely heal us all. Finally, I talked about all my challenges and how I was able to survive all. I believe God will do the same for anyone in a similar situation. All you have to do is trust Him. I trusted God through thick and thin, and it is my pleasure to tell you that "I survived."

With God, it will always be.

"VICTORY AT LAST"

About the Author

James C. Thomas, Sr. is a Chief Apostle in the Lord's Church. He currently serves as the Founder and Overseer of Chosen Generation Outreach International Ministries. Inc.

Apostle James C. Thomas, Sr. enjoys teaching and developing future spiritual leaders that are on the local, national, and international level. He draws his strength from the chosen assignment from God and fro the love of his family.

Apsostle Thomas, Sr. has been married to his wife for going on over 38 years. Together they have three childen.